• POEMS & PIECES •
• FOR ALL •

· ACKNOWLEDGEMENTS ·

I WISH to make the following acknowledgements to those who have helped me in the production of this book by way of sponsorship, photocopying, supplying photographs, research, and proof-reading, etc.

The RAF

Ransomes, Sims and Jefferies Ltd.

Farming Press Ltd.

Old Fox Clubhouse, Stowmarket

Munton and Fisons Ltd.

R. C. Knights and Sons, Stowmarket

Port of Felixstowe

Stowmarket Middle School

Boots, Stowmarket

Scottish Tourist Board

POEMS & PIECES FOR ALL

RAY CHAPLIN

Published October 1995 by
Cow and Calf Press
Ray and Sandra Chaplin
Sloe Farm
Straight Road · Battisford
Stowmarket
Suffolk
IP14 2HR

Also available by the same author:
"Poems and Meditations"
and
"Poems and Pictures for the Young"
from the above address

All Origination by
Settle Graphics
Settle
North Yorkshire
BD24 9BL

I.S.B.N. 0 9526766 0 5

Printed by
Pioneer Press Limited
Skipton
North Yorkshire
BD23 1JU

· CONTENTS ·

CONTINUED OVERLEAF

POEMS AND PIECES RELATING TO CHRISTIAN EXPERIENCE

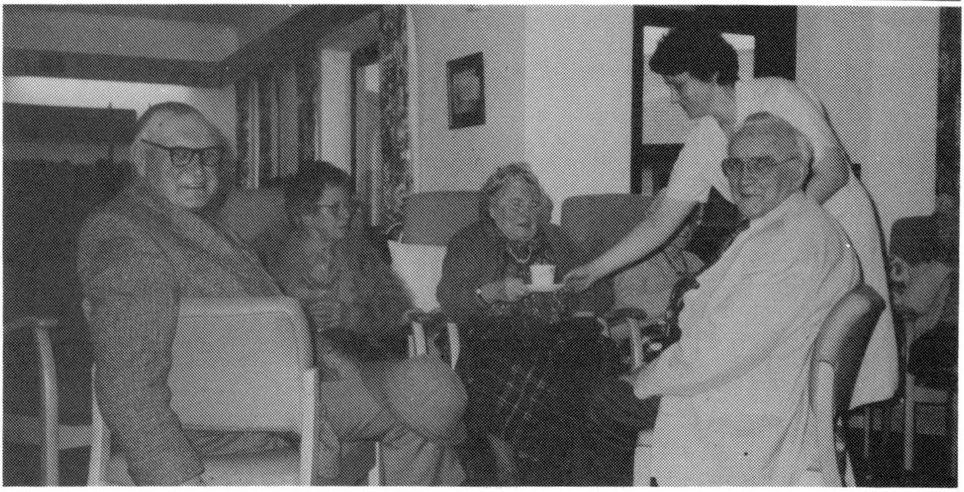

POEMS AS PRAYERS

• INTRODUCTION •

WHEN a friend kindly published my first book of poems in 1990 some wondered whether there would be much interest in the work because of the spiritual darkness of the days we are living in. Thankfully through the goodness of the LORD we have actually had many encouragements and sometimes, as a result of giving booklets away to schools and hospital wards, orders have come in from various places.

Since retiring from a farming partnership in 1991 due to health problems, I have been able to give more time to writing and now publish this third booklet. Through studying some of the great events that have taken place in our nation and

writing about them I have been stirred by the manifold mercies which God has granted us in our British Isles. I trust that others who may peruse these pages will also be moved in their hearts, and that these little pieces will interest many of all ages.

I am greatly indebted to my wife and family for their patience in helping me with this book, and am grateful again for the services of a good friend from Yorkshire as my typesetter whose excellent work speaks for itself.

I trust this book will find many interested readers, and God's Name will be glorified as a result.

Ray Chaplin

OUR front cover picture shows how men involved with the Rescue Services work together to save people whose lives have been threatened by unforeseen circumstances. Stories could be told of how pilots and lifeboatmen have risked their own lives so that other lives could be saved. Sometimes severe weather conditions and hazards such as fire have to be faced if people in great danger are to be brought to a place of safety.

Thinking about these matters reminds me of what a wonderful thing it is to be safe in one's soul and to have the assurance that though punishment in hell is what one really deserves, the work of the Saviour, the LORD JESUS, as He died upon the cross, secures the forgiveness of all of the sins of those who look to Him alone for mercy. Such mercy, however, is only for those who acknowledge that they cannot do anything to save themselves; those that come humbly through faith unto God to seek that grace which can take away our iniquities and clothe us with Christ's righteousness.

Sometimes when a swimmer is in difficulty and help is at hand, that person may struggle, as if wanting to do something to save himself. In that case the drowning man may have to be almost knocked out so that he may entirely rest upon the skill and ability of the lifesaver. What a picture this is of how we must acknowledge that all our efforts to get to Heaven are futile and cannot in any way procure for us Divine favour. No, we must accept that salvation is all of the LORD, and just as so many acknowledge that they owe so much to the Rescue Services for saving their lives, so may we, if we are now safe in our souls, continually thank God for giving His Son to come as a Saviour and Redeemer to save His people from their sins.

Poems About Places

• *England* •

Oh England, favoured of the LORD,
'Bove many lands with bounty stored
And full of history which may cause
Some foreign lands to stop and pause,
As they behold how from our soil
Men have arisen and through their toil
Achievements great have here been wrought
Which fame have in their wake us brought —
Consider Who has made thee great
And kept back foes from many a state,
Who would have plunged thee into grief,
Had not thy God sent thee relief.
Oh England! stop and think again,
Look to your past, and realise then
That if we would here blessed be
We must again from Scripture see
That we've provoked our God through sin
And passed wrong laws and gloried in
Much evil practice on God's day
And crimes adulterous now we say
Cannot be bad, since we may do
Whate'er we fancy — therefore who
Another's wife may wish to take
May break their oath for pleasure's sake.
Yet what a solemn attitude
And cause of many a family feud.
For God through every curtain sees
And such things surely Him displease.
Then hearken Britain's favoured sons,
Oh listen all ye troubled ones;
For if ye would here blessed be
The Bible open up and see
What grief must come to those who close
Its pages and her ways oppose.
So turn to God again and pray
For mercy — lest, our debt to pay,
Condemned in hell we for our shame
Should be confined through our own blame.

• NOTABLE EVENTS •

A BRIEF SUMMARY OF A FEW NOTABLE EVENTS OF BRITISH HISTORY OVER THE PAST FIVE HUNDRED YEARS

1476 Printing introduced into England by William Caxton.

1492 William Tyndale born (approx.). Translates the Bible into English. He was strangled and burnt at Vilvorde, Belgium, in 1536.

1588 Defeat of the Spanish Armada by the British Navy and Sir Francis Drake. Philip II of Spain wanted to make England Roman Catholic against the will of the Protestants of the British Isles, but many of the 130 or so vessels of the Armada, with their soldiers and instruments of torture, perished because of the expertise of our navy and a strong wind sent in God's mercy which scattered them. England was saved from a terrible invasion. The Spanish Armada was first spotted from a look-out post at Aldeburgh in Suffolk.

1605 The discovery and defeat of the Gunpowder Plot. Its conspirators wanted to destroy the British Protestant Parliament by setting light to barrels of gunpowder in the cellars of the Houses of Parliament. The plot was discovered on November 5th. We still celebrate this remarkable deliverance with bonfires and fireworks on Guy Fawkes day. Guy Fawkes was one of the leaders of this Jesuit plot.

1620 Voyage of the "Mayflower" to the New World.

1653 Commencement of the government of Oliver Cromwell (1653-1658).

1685 Many Huguenots (French Protestants) flee to England to escape persecution and bring with them skills in craftsmanship, especially textile manufacture. Many British families are able to trace their ancestry back to the Huguenots.

1688 William of Orange, at the request of many, landed at Torbay in Devon with a determination to maintain the Protestant religion and the liberties of England.

1690 James II defeated by William of Orange at the Battle of Boyne in Northern Ireland. William's reign was one of considerable progress in real liberty and he is ranked amongst historians as being one of our ablest kings.

1698 Thomas Savery invented a crude steam engine.

1726 George Frederick Handel granted British citizenship.

1729 Men such as Whitefield and the Wesleys meet up at university and become preachers who transform the lives of thousands in the nation. Historians have stated that through their preaching England was saved from the bloody revolution taking place at that time in France. George Whitefield had a very powerful voice that could clearly be heard two miles away and sometimes preached to as many as 40,000 in the open air. Miners from around Bristol were seen with channels down their grimy faces as the power of the preaching of God's Word brought tears to their eyes, and conviction and comfort to their hearts.

1781 George Stephenson born, engineer and builder of the first successful steam locomotive.

1796 Edward Jenner discovers how to innoculate against smallpox.

1797 Battle of St. Vincent.

1805 Battle of Trafalgar.

1809 Charles Darwin born who wrote a book on evolution. Before he died he rejected the theories of his book.

1827 Birth of photography.

1838 Great Western Paddle Steamer crosses the Atlantic in under 20 days.

1839 Admiralty orders its first iron naval steamer.

1840 The Penny Post introduced, helped by the railways.

1842 Shaftesbury's Bill forbad children under ten to work in mines.

1846 The first anaesthetics used successfully.

1876 Telephone invented.

1883 First electric tram in service.

1899 First motor bus in service.

1900 Marconi and others begin to develop radio and broadcasting (date is approximate).

1908 Model T Fords produced.

1914 Commencement of the First World War (1914-1918).

1929 Discovery of penicillin.

1939 Commencement of the Second World War (1939-1945).

1953 Queen Elizabeth crowned.

1969 Concorde's supersonic maiden flight.

1973 Three-day working week introduced due to oil shortage.

1982 The Falklands War.

1987 Hurricane hits Southern England — seventeen die, 15 million trees lost, and many homes destroyed.

1989 A total of 1,612 die in Britain from AIDS.

1990 The Government allocates £2.2 million to research Bovine Spongiform Encephalopathy ("Mad Cow Disease").

1994 The first train journey from England to France as the Channel Tunnel is opened.

1994 Thanksgiving services take place to mark the fiftieth anniversary of D Day. Some veteran soliders once again land in Normandy by parachute as part of the celebrations and speak of many of their comrades who died whilst advances were taking place which led, in God's mercy, to our ultimate victory in the Second World War.

• THE MONARCHY •

KINGS AND QUEENS OF ENGLAND SINCE 1461

	House of York
1461-1483	Edward IV
1483	Edward V
1483-1485	Richard III

	House of Tudor
1485-1509	Henry VII
1509-1547	Henry VIII
1547-1553	Edward VI
1553-1558	Mary Tudor
1558-1603	Elizabeth I

	House of Stuart
1603-1625	James I
1625-1649	Charles I
1660-1685	Charles II
1685-1688	James II
1689-1702	William III
1702-1714	Queen Anne

	House of Hanover
1714-1727	George I
1727-1760	George II
1760-1820	George III
1820-1830	George IV
1830-1837	William IV
1837-1901	Victoria

	House of Saxe-Coburg-Gotha
1901-1910	Edward VII

	House of Windsor
1910-1936	George V
1936	Edward VIII
1936-1952	George VI
1952-	Elizabeth II

• SUFFOLK •

SUFFOLK is both a delightful and historic county full of beauty which continues to fascinate tourists year after year. It covers an area of about 1,470 square miles. John Constable and Thomas Gainsborough, the well known painters, were both born in Suffolk, and people often speak about the East Bergholt area (Constable's birthplace) as being "Constable Country". The village of Lavenham was once a medieval wool town and still there are many old timbered houses which make this place well worth a visit. When Flemish weavers settled in England in the 14th century, Lavenham was already busy producing and exporting wool. William Gurnall, who wrote a well known book entitled "The Christian in Complete Armour", was a minister here in the largest parish church in West Suffolk, from 1644 to 1679.

The sea has long been an enemy of Suffolk and part of its coast has been eroded away. At one time Dunwich was an important port, but now it has sadly disappeared. In 1953 there was serious flooding around Felixstowe with the loss of over forty lives. This happened on the last day of January and some people who were housed in "pre-fabs" climbed helplessly onto their roofs, but were drowned before those in boats could rescue them. On a brighter note, though, you can now benefit at Felixstowe from one of the most modern ports in Europe. Many products are imported and exported through the docks here, and in 1993 over one million containers were handled.

In Suffolk there are several market towns. At Bury St. Edmunds, Lacy Scott, an old established firm of auctioneers, sell about 2,000 pigs, 300 cattle and 200 sheep each Wednesday. Poultry, wood, cars and bicycles are also sold by auction and help to create an interesting atmosphere amongst people with various accents. Also on Mondays, Lacy Scott hold a market at Wickham Market. Livestock markets used to be held at Ipswich, Sudbury and Stowmarket, but they all closed down in recent years. The main rivers are the Stour, which forms the boundary with Essex; the Waveney, which forms the boundary with Norfolk; the Blyth, Alde, Deben and Orwell. The coastline is 62 miles long.

The town of Hadleigh in Suffolk was noted for being very appreciative of the Bible when it was first translated, and apparently many of its inhabitants memorised much of it by heart because it was so precious to them. A former rector of Hadleigh, whose name was Roland Taylor, along with others in Suffolk, suffered as a martyr at the time when Mary Tudor was on the throne. They were regarded as heretics because they would not accept that masses were necessary for our salvation, and maintained that we are justified by faith alone through Christ alone as the Scriptures affirm (Romans 1:16-17). Much has been written about these martyrs who, whilst even being burnt at the stake, triumphed joyfully over their afflictions and shamed those who opposed them.

Suffolk is well known for its non-conformist places of worship. Many of these have been built over the last 200 years especially, and each Lord's Day there are still a goodly number who love to join with others to acknowledge and worship the One on whom we all depend. Some of these places of worship are rather obscurely situated and there are a few where nearby sheds tell of a time when they were used as stables by those who came by pony and trap. Many would bring their lunch with them. Others would walk through fields and woods, and cross over stiles leading off from meadows so that they could benefit from preaching on the Sabbath Day. Still today in Suffolk there are, by comparison with other counties, many who desire to follow in the ways of men and women of days gone by, who sought to honour God and humbly obey Him, and who called the Sabbath Day a delight.

In Suffolk there is a lot of good agricultural land well suited to growing wheat, barley and sugar-beet. During the 1993-1994 season 400,000 tonnes of sugar were produced. At the Ipswich sugar-beet factory approximately 425 lorry loads of beet are delivered each day during the campaign which starts in September and usually lasts about 120 days. Farms today have fewer workers than was the case a few decades ago. Older labourers sometimes speak of how they would be involved with a gang of eight or ten and would spend many hours hand hoeing. This may sound laborious work — and doubtless it was — but it seems that sometimes on Mondays they would discuss sermons they had heard the day before in different parishes, and as they laboured with their hands they were passing the time profitably, sanctifying their souls at the same time. Horsemen would have to be up very early and would take pride in grooming their animals and preparing the harness required for the particular season's work; there was quite a close relationship between horse and horseman. A story was once told of a stallion and wagon being left outside the Pickerel Inn at Stowmarket with the reins just left untied on the ground. When it was suggested to the horseman that someone would go off with this particular stallion, he told the person concerned to go and try — but the horse refused to move! "Prince" and "Duke" were common names for horses, along with "Diamond" and "Judy". Horses were taught to respond to various commands such as "Gee-up", "Waardee" (go to the right) and "Coppie Waardee" (come to the left) — these commands, however, varied from place to place. Suffolk horses were first bred at the end of the 18th century and were ideal for ploughing because they are without "feather" (a formation of hair) on their legs.

There are many lovely woods in Suffolk and some interested in birds have recorded beautiful dawn choruses on tape. A lot of oak wood, that was used for the first Royal Exchange in London, was grown on farms in the county.

Doubtless some of the atmosphere of rural Suffolk has gone in the name of progress, but there is still much remaining today that is both interesting and fascinating, making this part of the world special to many.

• Suffolk •

In England, down by the south east,
A county can be found,
With pretty villages and ponds,
Where farms and woods abound.

Here bounteous crops of wheat are grown
In soil which suits them well;
And labourers in our countryside
Have many a tale to tell.

The "Red Poll Cow" and "Suffolk Horse"
Have been made famous here,
And still are bred and sold to some
From places far and near.

The flocks of "Suffolk Sheep" here graze
And do our countryside
Enhance; then wool and lamb we have,
Which they for us provide.

Fine churches large and small here stand
And testimony bear
To some whose preaching still today
Through books they with us share.

In Hadleigh, Roland Taylor lived,
And for his stand became
A martyr, who when burnt to death,
Could glory in Christ's Name.

Yes, God in Suffolk has us blessed
With many godly men,
And many long that Bible truths
Might here be known again.

At Kersey right across the road
A stream you can see flow,
Where cottages unique still stand
And tourists come and go.

Much industry in towns you find
Where some machines are made;
Then Coxes apples too are grown
And in shops are displayed.

One factory where many work
Makes paint, which day by day
A sparkle brings to many homes
Through men skilled in this way.

To Suffolk's coastline many go
To take a holiday,
And near the Port of Felixstowe
Ships travel on their way.

The Queen some visits here has paid,
When crowds turned out to greet
Her Majesty, and let her know
We felt this was a treat.

Yes, Suffolk is a charming spot —
And meadows, lanes and trees,
Make me so glad God set me here,
Where so much does me please.

And still I trust on "Suffolk Soil"
Men will to God give praise,
And seek to do what pleases Him
Throughout their earthly days.

• LONDON •

IT was in the year AD 43 that Londinium, which we now call London, was named by the Romans. The city of London has probably had a greater influence on the world than any other city. Tourists of all nationalities find in our capital so much to interest them. There is still much that is unique about London and by visiting museums, observing the pageantry, and witnessing memorials which record remarkable events of yesteryear, one can observe some of the ways in which God has blessed this land like no other. Much of the prosperity that has come to London is, of course, related to the River Thames which, if it could speak, would have many exciting tales to tell of adventures which have either commenced or been continued from this spot. Like all cities London has had times of trial and uncertainty when its inhabitants have been brought very low. Through a well known rhyme children are helped to remember two dates in particular about our capital:

In 1665 there was hardly anybody left alive;
In 1666 London burned like rotten sticks.

At the time of the plague one person out of every five died — altogether about one million succumbed to the disease. People put a big red cross on their doors and wrote, "LORD have mercy upon us". One of the reasons why the plague spread so rapidly was because sanitation arrangements in those days were very inadequate. When the Great Fire struck London some felt that it was a blessing in disguise because people began to pay more attention to their homes and how they were built. The fire actually started in Pudding Lane in a baker's shop one Sunday morning; it was spread by a strong east wind and in four days 13,200 houses and 87 churches were reduced to ashes. Two million were made homeless.

Since the Great Fire of London there have been great improvements in the buildings of London. Sir Christopher Wren, through his expertise as an architect, has left us a wonderful heritage with the churches that he built; St. Paul's Cathedral, of course, being the most well known. In spite of the Second World War, which caused much havoc in London — when, for instance, in just one day 900 German aircraft came over in waves and bombed the docks and the East End in particular — many buildings of important historical interest may still be seen. Westminster Chapel, which is not far away from St. James' Park, proved a spiritual home to many. Some people came into this place from the City and many other parts of the world, and went out with changed hearts and a thankful spirit through the preaching of Dr. Martyn Lloyd Jones (1899-1981), who was used in a remarkable way as a faithful preacher of the truths of the Bible.

Space forbids us mentioning many building and places of interest, but Buckingham Palace is a good place to catch a glimpse of members of the Royal Family as they return or leave in one of the Rolls-Royces owned by the Sovereign. Many important engagements take place at Buckingham Palace. Other heads of state are often entertained here and around 400 servants are employed in a multitude of tasks involving many different talents.

Many people commute to London from the South and even from places as far away as Norwich and beyond, for there are numerous financial and banking organisations which, in spite of the advance of computers, still need many employees.

London's transport systems are kept very busy and carry over five million people daily. The world's first underground line was opened between Baker Street and the City in 1863, and since then many miles of track have been laid to help businessmen, tradesmen and tourists alike. Doubtless while time continues London will always be a place where adventures and achievements will be commemorated, and may there yet be many who will have more stories to tell of God's blessing upon London.

• *London* •

When tourists visit our fine land
And want to see around,
In London they should spend some time,
Where buildings grand are found.

For here our Queen lives, near Hyde Park
Her palace one can view,
With guards in splendid uniform
And boots that look brand new.

Then by "Big Ben" at Westminster
So many love to come,
Where acts and laws are passed and sealed
Affecting every home.

The Abbey can be seen near here,
Where kings and queens are crowned;
In history books tales of this place
Most certainly abound.

Saint Paul's Cathedral never fails
To interest passers-by,
And from its towers one much can view
From balconies up high.

Great Weddings here have taken place
And tombstones are displayed
Of naval lords who for our land
To fight were not afraid.

Upon the Thames a river trip
Can most instructive be,
'Neath bridges famous one may pass
And many landmarks see.

At Kensington museums there are
Which will one fascinate;
Of past achievements one can learn
That once made Britain great.

Fine music in our capital
In concert halls is played;
From here "The Proms" are broadcast live
As melody is made.

Yes, visitors to London find
They so much here may learn,
And kind policemen will them guide
If they have missed a turn.

And still I trust there will arise
From this fine city here,
Men of renown and uprightness
As year succeeds to year.

• SCOTLAND •

IN Scotland one may find some of the most magnificent scenery of the entire British Isles. From this part of the globe there have arisen great preachers, statesman, missionaries, soldiers, scientists and surgeons. The Scots are inveterate travellers and in many places one can find Caledonian clubs where they like to meet. Scotland can be divided into three parts: the Northern Highlands, the Central Lowlands, and the Southern Uplands.

Of Scotland's 19,500,000 acres, 15,000,000 are devoted to agriculture, which is one of the most important industries, where oats, barley and potatoes are the main crops. As far as livestock is concerned, Aberdeen Angus cattle have been exported all over the world and beef from this breed is still much sought after, in spite of the fact that many continental breeds are now becoming more popular. From the herds of Ayrshire cows some tasty cheeses are produced as well as many other dairy products. Highland cattle on bleak hillsides have attracted the attention of many an artist. On 12th August many Englishmen head north for grouse shooting as the season commences. Fishing boats go out from many ports and in Scottish waters catches are to be had of herring, haddock, cod, skate, and halibut. The Edinburgh International Festival has brought fame to Scotland and takes place in late August and September.

For many centuries the Sabbath Day has been special in these parts, but sadly much now takes place which is contrary to the Fourth Commandment. In many places, though, it is still possible to join with those who fear God in little churches where the Psalms are sweetly sung unaccompanied and the LORD is honoured as the only true and living God.

Here is a brief list of some famous people from Scotland:

John Knox (c. 1514-1572)
was a very clever student who studied at St. Andrew's University. He was brought up at a time when church services were held in Latin and thought that by good works he could obtain favour with God and earn salvation. However, he was brought to rejoice in the truth of the Bible and came to know Christ as Saviour. Through his preaching and work he accomplished great things for Scotland though opposed by some, notably Mary Queen of Scots, who was said to be more afraid of his preaching and prayers than all the armies of France.

William Murdoch (1754-1839)
was the first to use coal gas for lighting.

John McAdam (1756-1836)
did much to improve hard-wearing road surfaces.

Thomas Telford (1757-1834)
was responsible for the construction of more than 1,000 miles of road, 1,200 bridges, plus harbours, and churches, etc. He also helped with many major works in England.

James Tyler
became Great Britain's first aeronaut in 1784 by making an ascent from Edinburgh.

Robert Liston (1794-1847)
was the first to use a general anaesthetic.

Mrs. James Keiller
invented marmalade in 1797.

James Young (1811-1883)
was the first man to produce oil commercially.

Robert Murray M'Cheyne (1813-1843)
in his brief life was made a great blessing to many through his preaching; his sermons are still published today, as are some of his hymns. He saw God work in revival power in Dundee and spent some time working in Palestine as a missionary to the Jews.

David Livingstone (1813-1873)
was a famous missionary and during several journeys through Africa discovered the Victoria Falls.

John Thomson (1822-1892)
invented the refrigerator.

John Boyd Dunlop (1840-1921)
developed the pneumatic tyre.

Alexander Graham Bell (1847-1922)
was the inventor of the telephone.

Sir Alexander Fleming (1881-1955)
during a distinguished career discovered penicillin and pioneered several other treatments.

• *Scotland* •

Oh Scotland, how I love that land
With lochs and hillsides bleak,
Where lovely accents I enjoy
When people to me speak;
And on its mountains sure one finds
A lovely atmosphere,
Where one vast spaces can explore
And feel that God is near.

One island which I love right well
Up in these northern parts
Is Arran, and so many folk
Have memories in their hearts
Of walks enjoyed here, when they have
God's handiworks espied;
Where Highland cattle they have watched
Upon the mountainside.

Brave men in Scotland have been born
And served their people well.
John Knox was one who loved God's Word,
Whose voice no one could quell.
For he opposed all popish ways
Within his native land,
And for the Bible's blessed ways
He made a fearless stand.

One grand event I have enjoyed,
Near an old castle's walls,
Is the "tattoo", when bands and pipes
Obey their captain's calls;
And splendid music well rehearsed
At this spot you can hear.
The fine displays make this for some
A highlight of the year.

Besides the scenery of this land,
Where many do return,
Because they love the peace there found
Near stream and hill and burn;
Of haggis some do love to taste
And porridge brewed so well —
Here made from oats which farmers grow,
Then to their merchants sell.

Yes, Scotland is a lovely part
Of our fine British Isles,
And friendly people there I meet,
Welcome me with their smiles;
And may much blessing here be known
And righteousness exalt
Her people midst its lochs and braes
In settings there unspoilt.

• YORKSHIRE •

THE largest county in England, Yorkshire possesses an atmosphere all of its own. Many tourists and holidaymakers spend time here and return with vivid memories of interesting places and people, and spectacular views which take one's breath away.

The Yorkshire Dales are noted for their dry-stone walls, farm houses, cottages and barns. Many of the walls, which have faced up well to the rigours of severe winters, have been used by several generations to seperate flocks of sheep and cattle found in abundance in this northern county. Swaledale and Teeswater sheep can be seen grazing on the steeper hills, and in some valleys newer breeds such as Texels are kept. Aberdeen Angus cattle seem to be quite popular, as they are shorter on the leg, which can be an advantage when they are housed in a small barn. More recently developed breeds of cattle are now being reared on upland pastures, such as the Belgian Blue and the Charolais, which are often crossed with more traditional breeds. Sadly, however, the demand for lamb and beef nowadays is not always so encouraging — many seem to ignore the fact that it was God who gave us meat to enjoy. It is fascinating to watch a farmer call his stock from afar, in accents and expressions best understood by the animals! Yorkshire has many becks (streams) and rivers, so finding water for the stock is not a big problem.

A ride on the Settle-Carlisle Railway line ("The Long Drag") is a good way of seeing some of the most wonderful scenery in Yorkshire. This line was constructed between 1869 and 1876 and was very difficult to build. Not a few of the navvies (or labourers) sadly lost their lives whilst building the line, both by accident and outbreak of disease emanating from the somewhat primitive and uncomfortable camps where the men were staying. This famous line almost closed down in 1989, but public opinion and the efforts of railway enthusiasts prevailed, and there was great delight when the announcement was made that it was to remain open. Steam trains often run along this well known route. In the York National Railway Museum is the famous "Mallard", which broke the world speed record for a steam locomotive — 126 m.p.h. At the same museum may be seen many old engines, carriages and exhibits from the golden age of steam.

Yorkshire is geologically full of interest and in recent years many underground caverns have been discovered. It is now possible to enjoy a guided tour and walk underground for half a mile at Whitescar Caves, Ingleton. Waterfalls, streams, stalactites and stalacmites, so fascinating to study, are found in abundance here. Unspoilt nature also provides the opportunity to reflect on the wonders of God's glorious creation.

Delicious Wensleydale cheese is produced in Hawes, where it is also possible to watch ropes being made — used not only by local farmers for haltering their animals or securing their loads of hay, but also specially produced ropes which act as barriers for stately homes. At Skipton it is possible to enjoy a ride on a barge along the canal or see the well-preserved 900-year-old castle. During the Civil War this was besieged for three years, the inhabitants being helped by an ancient well (uncovered in 1992). The well known local newspaper, The Craven Herald & Pioneer, has its offices here, along with the printing works which produces pamphlets and books that travel to many different places world-wide.

A town well worth a visit is Haworth, which stands on bleak moorland country on the hills dividing Yorkshire from Lancashire. In the parsonage during the last century lived the Brontë sisters, remembered for their literary ability. One can here enjoy a ride on a steam train along the Oxenhope to Keighley line, Britain's last remaining complete branch line railway. One man who laboured in Haworth in the middle of the 18th century, before travel by steam engine was possible and when communications were very slow, did much to benefit her inhabitants' souls. This was William Grimshaw, who was known throughout Yorkshire as the apostle of the district. He preached wherever he could get people together, in barns, fields, a quarry or by the roadside. He spoke plainly to people about their souls and multitudes began to think about their spiritual condition who had never thought about it before. He seldom preached less than twenty times a week and through his labours many were brought to know the joy of having their sins forgiven and were able to rejoice in possession of everlasting life through the mercy of Christ Jesus, who came into the world to save sinners. In spite of being persecuted, Grimshaw stood firm for the truths of God's Word. He was actually ordained as an unconverted man, but following his conversion said it was as though God lifted up his Bible to Heaven and let down for him a new one. One feels it would be good if we could see such brave preachers being raised up in these days, who would point people to the answer to their heart's need.

So much is of interest in Yorkshire that space does not permit the mentioning of many places, which from a historical, educational and informative point of view, have so much to tell. One cannot do better than to spend a week or two in this beautiful part of the world, admiring the lovely dales, moors, hills and rivers, which all combine to offer a break for those who seek a place far from the madding crowd.

• *North Yorkshire* •

North Yorkshire is a lovely place
To come and stay a while.
Its people friendly are and they
Will greet you with a smile.

The scenery is in a class
Distinctly of its own,
And walks and views you can enjoy
In hills, dales, moors and town.

What lovely landscapes you can view
When it is bright and clear,
And oft you find on hills in mist
A pleasant atmosphere.

The Settle-Carlisle railway line
In these parts you will find,
And there a trip you can enjoy
Which will stick in your mind.

Yes, in these parts there is so much
You can enjoy and see;
So try it out and you will find
That you've been blessed — like me.

• RAF WATTISHAM •

(NOW CALLED WATTISHAM AIRFIELD)

THE construction of the base at Wattisham (which is just a mile away over the fields from my home) commenced in 1937, when 4.4 hectares of land were purchased to develop an airfield. Over the next two years a further 182 hectares changed hands and land that had been used for farming now became host to aircraft of the RAF. Originally there were only grass runways. The first bombing raid of the Second World War left from Wattisham, when Bristol Blenheims were used. Wing Commander Oswald Gayford was the first commander. As a gifted pilot he actually set a world record in February 1933, flying a Fairey Monoplane from Cranwell, Lincolnshire, to Walvis Bay in South Africa, in 57 hours and 25 minutes. The distance travelled in this non-stop flight was 5,307 miles.

In 1942 the station was used by the 8th Air Force of the USAAF and hardened runways were built. P38 J Lightnings flew from Wattisham at this time — not to be confused, however, with the English Electric Lightning, which didn't arrive until 1960. After the war and right through to the 1950s aircraft such as Spitfires, Meteors (one of the first jets), Ansons, Chipmunks, Vampires and Javelins could be seen parked in the hangers at Wattisham.

In 1958 the famous Black Arrows Display Team made its home at the base. This famous group thrilled the crowds, especially by their unsurpassed ability to perform a twenty-two aircraft loop.

In 1960 Wattisham was favoured to be the home for the English Electric Lightnings of 56 and 111 Squadrons. These remained in service for fifteen years, followed in 1975 by McDonnell Douglas Phantom FGR2s, which continued to play their part in the defence of our shores. The Phantom aircraft was decommissioned in 1992 and the base handed over to 3 Regiment Army Air Corps. Now Wattisham opens up another chapter of its history with Nos. 653, 662 and 663 Squadrons flying Gazelle and Lynx helicopters. Also currently based here are two Sea King helicopters, serving with B Flight 22 Squadron. These are ready to help with certain emergencies which may arise anywhere from The Wash right down to Beachy Head. The Sea Kings have a crew of four and can remain airborne for about six hours.

• RAF Wattisham •

Since all my life from near my farm
I have been pleased to see
The aircraft of the RAF
Take off and land near me,
I think I'll miss them when they go,
For they have now become
As friends whose company I enjoy
When working at my home.

Sad moments I can now recall,
When crashes there have been,
And once a Javelin hit the ground,
Then smoke and flames were seen.
But though some pilots have been killed
And sadness we have known,
Not many aircraft have been lost
Of all those that have flown.

This friend was once at my small church
Engaged to come and preach,
But at the time was posted north —
And so he could us reach
His Lightning he did use that he
Might still God's Word proclaim,
Which cheered our hearts, and this event
Rare history became.

At Wattisham it's great to watch
A plane from Q.R.A.*
Come into action with great skill,
Then orders soon obey.
Such things do almost make me proud
To live in this our land,
Where God has many brave men given,
Who do for justice stand.

The Lightning aircraft was, I thought,
A plane both fast and grand,
And could so quickly leave the ground,
Though soon it had to land —
Unless refuelling could take place,
Which meant it far could fly,
And warn intruders round our shores
Of boundaries in the sky.

A Lightning pilot known to me
Did once quite calmly say,
That out to Cyprus he could fly
And back the selfsame day;
His breakfast he would eat at home,
Then he could dine out there —
But soon be back at Wattisham,
With friends his tea to share.

Since Phantoms have for many years
Been busy at our base,
And service good have to us given,
I hope still at this place
That other aircraft from this spot
Will serve our country well,
That children growing up may yet
Have many a tale to tell.

* Quick Reaction Alert.

• HADLEIGH SHOW •

THE first minute book of the Hadleigh Farmers' Agricultural Association states that the first annual subscription for members, which allowed them to attend the annual show, was two shillings — now the equivalent of 10p. How inflation has changed things since those early days! When shows were first held, motorised transport was, of course, virtually non-existent, but horses and carts carrying all sorts of produce would wend their way from outlying villages to display and compete for a prize, ploughs would be brought from quite a distance sometimes, and on fields around Hadleigh competitions would take place. In those days farmers would have some fallow land which needed ploughing two or three times a year so that weeds could be kept to a minimum. This would have been before the days of modern weedkillers and sprays, and the ploughing that needed to be done helped to keep the younger horses in training between seedtime and harvest. Prizes were apparently very good in those early days and sometimes a figure of five pounds was mentioned, which must have sent some entrants home with a happy heart, even if their feet might have been rather weary.

In 1939, when the 100th show took place, a gentleman named Colonel Hitchcock wheeled a large gun on to the showground to mark the occasion, but upon being fired some livestock were rather alarmed, causing problems for the stockmen, who did not think this a very good idea! The day ended with a spectacular fireworks display.

Exhibitors at the Hadleigh Show often speak of how much they enjoy coming along to Holbecks Park to compete, where there is such a friendly environment. In recent years new breeds of livestock have been brought in to join the older breeds still exhibited at the show. In many ways our lovely Suffolk horses, which look so magnificent as they gently stride round the rings, still act as the stars of the show and help to create a lovely atmosphere in a superb part of our county. Here one can enjoy many of the glories of God's creation and behold the beauty that makes a day at the Hadleigh Show a treat to remember.

• The Hadleigh Show •

At Holbecks Park each year in May
A goodly crowd you'll see,
For here the Hadleigh Show is held,
Where trees and pastures be;
And midst those oaks and meadows green
My friends I love to join,
Where well-bred animals are found
With coats well groomed that shine.

And what an atmosphere you find,
Where so much you can view,
For in the rings parades take place,
Of tractors old and new;
There Suffolks pure you can observe
And stockmanship supreme;
Then some grand trophies here receive,
For which they once did dream.

When in and out of tents you walk,
What talents you behold,
Where art and crafts are on display,
By entrants young and old;
And flower arranging classes are
A fascinating sight,
Here gentle hands have laboured long
To set things out just right.

On some stands tractors are displayed,
All clean and painted bright —
Though farmers hesitate to buy
Unless the price is right.
But children sometimes stand and stare,
Imagining one day
They'll have a tractor of their own
To mow the fields of hay.

Much work, of course, is carried out
By stewards of the Show,
And some give time throughout the year
That things might be just so;
And gratitude we ought to show
To those who own the spot,
Which one glad Saturday in May
Brings joy to such a lot.

• THE GULF WAR •

THE Gulf War lasted from 17th January to 28th February 1991. It began by Iraq invading Kuwait, entirely unprovoked, on 2nd August 1990. The allied forces, mainly from the United States, faced Iraqi forces which on paper seemed formidable: about 350,000 Iraqi troops were occupying Kuwait. Of these, an estimated 100,000 were killed and 65,000 were captured. Allied losses in God's mercy were very low by comparison — 234 killed and 479 wounded. British aircraft, including Jaguars, Jump Jets and Tornados, played a key part in the conflict. The United States Stealth Fighter, which was developed with the purpose of being able to avoid radar recognition, was also active in this war.

• The Gulf War •

Now in the Gulf the guns are quiet,
How glad our spirits are,
For from oppression some are free,
Who see an end to war.

Yet what distress this strife has caused,
Brought on by pride and greed;
But God be praised for victory given
And help in time of need.

For though in conflict men are brave
And weapons use with skill,
Unless the LORD had mercy shown,
There could be fighting still.

How right it is then praise to give
To God for answering prayer;
And may His grace bereaved ones know,
Who grief and losses share.

Oh LORD, remind us through this war,
How soon our lives could end;
And teach us on Thy Name to call,
Who did a Saviour send.

And through this war bring many men
To know of sins forgiven;
Joys may they know, not known before,
And go at last to Heaven.

So through events out in the Gulf,
May good to souls thus come;
And soon in mercy bring our lads
In safety to their home.

• The Army •

(Daniel Chaplin, age 7)

When war was coming in Iraq,
The army overtook,
The planes were fighting all the time
And ships aboard the sea.

The army got in their big tanks
And came with their big guns,
But 'twas not us who won the war.
But God who helped so.

Poems About People

• ADAM AND EVE •

WHEN God created the world in six days, the first man he made was Adam. God set Adam in the Garden of Eden, where he gave names to all the animals which had been placed there. God saw that it was not good for the man to be alone and so He caused a deep sleep to fall upon Adam and took one of his ribs from which He made Eve to be a helpmeet for him.

When Adam and Eve were first made, they enjoyed sweet communion with the LORD and there was no sadness or distress whatsoever. They disobeyed the command of God, however, and listened to the devil who tempted them to taste the fruit from the one tree which God had forbidden them to eat from. By so doing they brought a curse upon themselves and all their posterity and even the earth now started to bring forth thistles and thorns such as had not been seen before. In great mercy God promised that there would be a Saviour, who in due time was to die upon a cruel cross as a sacrifice to take away the sins of those who trust in Him.

• *Adam and Eve* •

When in the Bible I am told
Of Adam, who with Eve of old,
On earth by God was set,
I wonder what their world was like
Ere Satan's tempting blows did strike,
What splendours they'd have met?

For sin had not their world defiled,
On them their God in mercy smiled
And all seemed bright and well;
Yet sadly Him they disobeyed
And then His anger was displayed
As they when tempted fell.

Indeed, 'tis true, if I'd been there,
I'd in that guilt and sorrow share,
Because of my bad heart;
But I'm so thankful God declared,
In words most precious from His Word,
Salvation He'd impart.

So now, in Christ, believers may
Know all their sin's been washed away,
By faith through God's free grace;
And soon in Heaven He will bestow
His glories to those who Him know
In that most wondrous place.

• JOSEPH •

WHEN Joseph was young he had some dreams which indicated that one day all his brothers would bow down to him. He received cruel treatment from them, for they were envious, and actually sold him as a slave. He was taken away from his home in Canaan to Egypt and served Potiphar, who was an officer to Pharoah. We read in Genesis chapter 39 that the LORD was with Joseph, however, and he became a prosperous man. Following promotion to overseer of the house of his master, Potiphar's wife tried hard to tempt and entice him, but he determined that he would not do that which was displeasing to God. This woman told lies about Joseph which led to his imprisonment, but even there he was a help to others when he interpreted the dreams of two of Pharaoh's servants as God enlightened him.

When Pharoah himself was troubled by dreams which no one could interpret, Joseph was called for and told him that God was going to send seven years of plenty upon the land, to be followed by seven years of famine. Joseph was exalted to a very high position and in wisdom oversaw the storing up of much corn in readiness for the lean years that were to follow. When the famine was affecting Joseph's own family, his brothers came to buy corn and although they had been so cruel to him, he completely forgave them and was very kind in seeing that his ageing father and all his loved ones now came to be with him. In God's providence Joseph was the one to whom many owned so much at a time of distress and famine.

• *Joseph* •

When Joseph tempted was to do
A thing wrong in God's sight,
He yielded not, but overcame,
And stood for what is right.

And though a wicked woman thought
He would in her delight,
He turned away and honoured God
And stood for what is right.

Though tempted for so many days,
To see if then he might
Do what so many would have done,
He stood for what is right.

Thus in these days when sin abounds
And darkness men call light,
May I, if tempted in this way,
Then stand for what is right.

So may I seek to turn from wrong,
Though hard might be the fight,
That I like Joseph honour God
And stand for what is right.

(Genesis 39:7-20)

• JOB •

JOB was a prosperous man who suddenly found himself facing terrible trials, but manifested a strong faith in God. In one day he lost his ten children, his oxen, sheep and camels. He was also troubled by much physical distress. At one point his wife told him to "curse God, and die", but he replied: "Shall we receive good at the hand of God, and shall we not receive evil?" Certain friends tried to comfort Job, but they did not really help him very much. At the end of the book that bears his name we read about the Lord blessing the latter end of Job more than the beginning, for he had 14,000 sheep, 6,000 camels, 1,000 yoke of oxen, and 1,000 she asses. Also he had seven sons and three daughters.

• *Job* •

Amongst the people in God's Word
That I do read about,
For trials and sufferings they endured,
Job certainly stands out.

Because in one day he did lose
His sons and herds and flock,
But he was kept from murmuring free,
Though Satan did him mock.

And so strong was his trust in God,
"For He," said Job, "did give:
And may He not then take away
Before whom we do live?"

Then when he was afflicted sore
And pain acute he knew,
Upward he looked and comfort found
By keeping God in view.

So when like Job I losses know,
Which threaten faith to shake,
May I still hold fast and then prove
God will not me forsake.

Thus may my friends around me see
That precious is my LORD,
And honour then be brought to Him
Through grace He did afford.

• ABRAHAM •

ABRAHAM is called in Scripture the "father of the faithful". God made a promise to him that from his seed there would arise a great nation. For many years Abraham and his wife were without a child, but eventually they were blessed with Isaac, who was born miraculously when Sarah was past normal child-bearing age. In Genesis chapter 22 we read that God then tried Abraham's faith by commanding him to offer his son for a burnt offering upon a mountain. Although it must have been very difficult for him to obey the LORD, he made preparations, set out, and was about to slay his son when the angel of the LORD called unto him out of Heaven and told him not to lay his hand upon Isaac. At this point Abraham saw a ram caught in a thicket and offered this animal up instead of his son.

In the New Testament we are told of how Abraham was not justified in God's sight because of his works, but through his faith. The sacrifices of the Old Testament were instituted to teach people to look forward to the time when the LORD JESUS would die as the One Sacrifice, who would take away the sins of His people for ever. In Romans 4:20-25 we read that Abraham "staggered not at the promise of God through unbelief; but was strong in faith, giving glory to God; and being fully persuaded that, what He had promised, He was able to perform. And therefore it was imputed to him for righteousness. Now it was not written for his sake alone, that it was imputed to him; but for us, also, to whom it shall be imputed, if we believe on Him that raised up Jesus our Lord from the dead; who was delivered for our offences, and was raised again for our justification."

• *Abraham* •

When called to offer up his son
Was Abraham of old,
He trusted God and sought to do
Just as he had been told.

Although he knew not why the LORD
Did this command unfold,
He knew God's ways are best and did
Just as he had been told.

When Isaac asked why he could not
A lamb with knife behold,
He calm remained and purposed still
To do as he was told.

And through this trial he faith was given,
More precious than fine gold,
When God that ram gave he was glad —
And did as he was told.

And if believers had strong faith,
Which would their lives then mould,
Less doubt they'd have and more concern
To do the things they're told.

So as this godly man we still
In admiration hold,
May we in faith more humbly learn
To do the things we're told.

• C. H. SPURGEON •

CHARLES Haddon Spurgeon (1834-1892) was born at Kelvedon in Essex three years before William IV died and Queen Victoria commenced her long reign. During the time that he lived great strides were made in this country concerning medical knowledge and improvement on the railways, etc., although there were still many people who were very poor. Spurgeon was brought to know the LORD through listening to a simple preacher speak from Isaiah 45:22, where we read: "Look unto me, and be ye saved, all the ends of the earth: for I am God, and there is none else." He immediately was very keen to tell others about the wonderful Saviour he had found. Oportunities soon came his way to speak in humble cottages and barns. He walked many miles in this work and was made a great blessing to country folk. He became known as the boy preacher, and was called to be the minister at Waterbeach when only seventeen years of age. God used him here in remarkable ways and the village, once notorious for drunkenness and profanity, was transformed. Just two years later he was called to London, where he laboured faithfully until his death.

He preached to many thousands who flocked to hear him and loved to point sinners to the LORD JESUS as the only Saviour. During his life he published many books and his ministry was so valued that every Monday one of his sermons was published in a national newspaper. Spurgeon's writings are still read today all over the world.

• *Mr. C. H. Spurgeon* •

Amongst God's servants who have been
A blessing to our land,
Charles Haddon Spurgeon we revere,
Who for the truth did stand;
For when we hear of how he preached
And thousands who were saved,
Our hearts are thrilled, and for this man
We say, "God's Name be praised!".

We love to hear of how he came
At first to know the LORD,
And on one snowy morning went
Where he the Gospel heard;
And God a rustic preacher used,
So Spurgeon then did look
Unto the LORD who saved his soul
And all his sorrows took.

Then what a preacher he became,
For though in barn and home
He started preaching, through this youth
Men felt to them had come
God's Word in such a powerful way,
That sin to them became
A burden, so they Christ did seek,
And precious found His Name.

And when to London Spurgeon came,
So many help received,
And children helpless on the streets
Were cared for and relieved.
Then for young pastors there was built
A college, so that they
Instructed could be for their work,
And might God's Word obey.

And surely we are glad that though
A century has passed on,
Through Spurgeon's writings still today
Souls unto Christ are won;
And though we live in trying days,
When evil does abound,
His influence still is known by some
Who blessedness have found.

So as we think of how God used
This man for His own praise,
We long to see God's Spirit move
With power in these our days:
That once again in our loved land
Large numbers may appear
In churches, as in Spurgeon's day,
And God's Word truly hear.

• HORATIO NELSON •

NELSON was born in Norfolk and joined the navy at the age of twelve as a midshipman. He lost his right eye at Corsica in 1794. He was in command of a ship called "Captain" at the battle of Cape St. Vincent in 1797. At Santa Cruz he lost his right arm in action, but he was a very brave man and in 1798, when he was Rear Admiral, his fleet destroyed a French fleet in the Battle of the Nile. Only four ships escaped as Nelson captured seventeen other vessels. In 1801 he fought under Admiral Parker at Copenhagen. During the battle Parker signalled to Nelson to break off action, but Nelson put his blind eye to the telescope and said he did not see the signal, so carried on with the battle until he won. At this time he was made a Viscount.

In May 1803 he hoisted his flag on H.M.S. "Victory", which was at sea for two years searching for the French fleet. Nelson and his crew chased them to the West Indies and back to Cadiz. On the 21st October 1805 he met the French and Spanish fleet at Trafalgar. There he hoisted the signal: "England expects that every man will do his duty". The British fleet was in two columns. Before the battle someone suggested that he remove his medals in case an enemy spotted them because they were rather conspicuous. He replied, "That in honour he won them and in honour he wore them". However, it was probably these same medals which were spotted by an enemy who fired at Nelson from the "Redoubtable". Nelson died five hours later, but survived long enough to hear that England had won the battle. Only ten enemy ships escaped and none ever sailed again. The British fleet sustained 1,600 casualties; the combined French and Spanish fleet 14,000. As a result of the battle many men became deaf due to the noise of the gunfire. It is still possible to see the "Victory" today at Portsmouth.

Sadly, Nelson was not known for a godly life. However, in God's providence he was undoubtedly raised up to be a blessing to our country.

• *Lord Nelson* •

When England faced an awful foe,
Almost two hundred years ago,
From lands beyond our shore,
A gifted admiral God us gave,
Who through his navy did us save
From much bloodshed and war.

And though Trafalgar's battle was
A bloody conquest, all because
Of greed and lust for power,
Yet England's sailors Nelson hold
As a true hero, brave and bold,
Raised up for such an hour.

• H.M.S. ''VICTORY'' •

H.M.S. "Victory" was launched in 1765 as a first rate ship. Containing three decks, it was made of English oak, had 104 guns, three masts, was square rigged, and had a crew of 850 officers and men. The top of the main mast was 205 feet above the sea. Weighing 2,162 tons, "Victory" was 226 feet long and fought in the battles of St. Vincent and Trafalgar.

Nelson's crew were highly trained and could prepare for battle in six minutes. All the furniture was stored away, the boats towed astern, the decks sanded, and the guns prepared for action. The guns could fire 1½ miles and at a range of 500 yards the shot would pierce three feet of wood. Fifteen men had charge of two guns which fired many types of shot requiring a lot of powder. Approximately 50% of the crew were pressed, 22% volunteered and there were also some criminals. It took 140 men to weigh anchor; these were four in number and each weighed 84 cwt. When the hammocks were not used they were put in the netting. Thomas Hardy, who was the Captain, had his cabin at the stern.

The men had one hot meal a day. Half the crew had this in the morning and half in the evening. Although food was bad, rations were plentiful. Weekly rations were: 7 pounds of biscuits; 4 pounds of beef; 2 pounds of pork; 6 ounces of butter; 12 ounces of cheese; 2 pints of peas; 2 pints of oatmeal; 7 pints of beer; 14 gils of rum. The biscuits were hard and full of weevils, so they mashed them up until they came out! The animals lived on a lower deck and were slaughtered before a battle. The Orlop deck, below the water-line, was painted red, so that the blood from the wounded and those undergoing surgery — without anaesthetic — would not be noticed. It was here that Nelson died. Below this deck was the hold were stores were kept. At the very bottom was the ballast of shingle and iron bars.

The wages were: Boy £4 0s. 0d. per year; Seaman £1 5s. 0d. per month; Midshipman £1 5s. 6d. per month; Lieutenant £7 0s. 0d. per month; Captain £28 0s. 0d. per month; Lord Nelson £74 10s. 0d. per month.

• JOHN BUNYAN •

JOHN Bunyan's well known book, "The Pilgrim's Progress", has been translated many times down the years and there are even Eskimos who can read it in their own language. Probably the most popular devotional book ever written in English, it depicts the progress of Christian, who sets out on a journey with a burden of sin on his back, from the City of Destruction to the Celestial City. Although the story is told as though it was a dream, it comes across in such a moving way that many have cause to be thankful for this "Immortal Dreamer" — as Bunyan is sometimes called.

John Bunyan was born in 1628 and started life as a tinker (a mender of small metal utensils). He underwent deep conviction of sin before coming to know Christ as Saviour. He loved to preach about the way of salvation, but was imprisoned for so doing. It was in Bedford prison that he wrote "Pilgrim's Progress" and several other books, including an autobiography entitled "Grace Abounding to the Chief of Sinners". Though it must have been hard for Bunyan to have been in prison, in God's providence far more have been blessed through his writing than ever received help through his preaching.

• *John Bunyan* •

When Bunyan "Pilgrim's Progress" wrote
In Bedford's tiny jail,
He little thought that would become
A very well-known tale.
For many souls through reading this
Have come to trust the LORD,
And still today this book much good
Does unto men afford.

For Bunyan paints a picture true
About the Christian's life,
And with his characters he does
Speak of the pilgrim's strife.

Then he the reader does remind
That life a journey is,
And at the end each one will know
Eternal woe or bliss.

And whilst we Bunyan's Christian watch
Upon his pilgrim way,
So many aspects of God's Word
Still speak to us today;
And though the Christian life be hard,
The LORD God, who was made
To Bunyan precious in that jail,
Will still His people aid.

• THE INVENTOR •

In days when mass-produced motor cars are so common, it is easy to forget that not so long ago none had even heard of mass-production. Henry Ford (1863-1947) was the first man to think of using a conveyor belt to help mechanics assemble cars. This was in 1908. In nineteen years Ford made 15,000,000 Ford Model Ts and in 1941 helped the war effort by making bombers and tanks.

If we go back further to 1698, an Englishman called Thomas Savery invented a crude steam engine. James Watt (1736-1819) did much to improve the steam engine and went into partnership with Matthew Boulton, from Birmingham. Together they built the famous Boulton & Watt engines. James Watt also invented the slide valve and the governor. George Stephenson (1781-1848) is famous for his "Rocket", which achieved the then remarkable speed of 30 m.p.h. In the light of rail travel today it is hard to believe his contemporaries actually wondered whether the human body could stand up to travelling at that speed!

• *Transport and Travel* •

In days when travel has become
So quick, and we may from our home
Jump in a car, or bus, or train,
Or at an airport board a plane
To visit loved ones far away,
'Tis good to think of yesterday,
When men like Henry Ford began
To use their skills to build and plan.

For it is easy to forget
What trials our first inventors met,
When they with simple tools and steam
Turned to reality a dream,

So that the horse and cart so slow,
Might certain competition know,
Through work by Watts and Stephenson,
As forms of travel new began.

And now that man has reached the moon,
I guess that travelling very soon
New forms may take, as man does grow
In knowledge, and prowess does show.
And I feel favoured that I can
Be fascinated as men plan
For means of transport yet unknown,
Which soon may unto us be shown.

• WILLIAM TYNDALE •
• AND THE BIBLE •

WILLIAM Tyndale was born circa 1492 when there was much darkness and priestcraft in our land. People were ignorant concerning the needs of their souls, but Tyndale did much to forward the work of the Reformation through translating the Bible into English from the original texts. It was his desire that even the boy who followed the plough should be able to read the Scriptures, which are able to make one wise unto salvation through faith which is in Christ Jesus. Tyndale was persecuted by those who opposed the truths of the Bible and after fleeing to the Continent was strangled and burnt at the stake in 1536. He had commenced a great work, however, and people were very pleased that they could now go to churches and hear the Scriptures read. At first large Bibles were actually chained to lecterns.

For many years no other book in the English language has had such a great effect on the great and the lowly as the Bible. It has affected speech and character and once when Queen Victoria was asked for the secret of Britain's greatness, she pointed to a Bible in reply. Our attitude to God's Word will ultimately effect our destiny in the world to come.

Many scholars have set out to prove the Bible false and not only failed to achieve their purpose but have been brought to rejoice in the glorious truths contained therein. The message of the Bible, which sadly is so often despised today, is that God is the One who is exalted over all, and that though sin has effected everyone, yet there is a way whereby sinners can know cleansed and renewed hearts by turning to the LORD JESUS CHRIST, God's Son, who when He died upon a cross, became a substitute to atone for the sins of all His people.

Christians believe the Bible to be inspired and God-breathed — in other words, though it was men who wrote the words, yet they were prompted by the LORD Himself. One strong proof for the inspiration of the Bible is the fact that so many of the faults and failings of men are recorded in the Scriptures, whereas if men write about themselves, there is always a tendency to gloss over their own faults.

The Bible has brought great comfort to many in times of distress and trial. During the last war, certain Psalms were read again and again and the faith of some was strengthened in spite of their circumstances. Hymns which have been penned by others in times of distress also illustrate this truth.

More copies of the Bible have been sold down the years than any other book. If we think of the work of an organisation such as the Gideons it is interesting to note that they actually give away 1,000,000 Bibles every thirteen days. In countries which have recently been freed from Communism there is such a hunger for the Word of God that printers and Bible Societies are kept very busy seeking to meet this demand. How good it would be if once again the truths of the Bible were valued more in this land — then surely many of the problems that beset us now would no longer trouble our rulers. The same power that accompanied God's Word in days gone by is able to transform the lives of many in Great Britain again.

• William Tyndale •

When William Tyndale work began
To translate Scripture, and to plan
The way whereby the ploughboy might
Of Bible truths have some insight,
He faced so many foes who sought
To keep from men the truths he taught.
Yet faithfully he worked right on
And when he had his labours done,
Those ancient printing presses were
The way whereby men now could share
With one another truths Divine.
What light then did on England shine,
For men were shown that Christ alone
Can pardon sin, and guilt atone —
And oh that Scripture truths again
Might precious be to many men.

I will prayse the O lorde/that though
thou were angrye with me/yet thyne an
ger is turned/and thou hast comforte
me. Beholde God is my saluacion: I will be
bolde therfore and not feare. For the lorde
God is my strength and my prayse wherof
I synge: and is become my savyoure. And ye
shall drawe water in gladnes oute of the wel
les of saluacion. And ye shall saye in that da
ye: geve thankes unto the lorde/ call on his na
me: make his dedes knowen amonge the he=
then: remember that his name is hie. Lyfte
up. Synge unto the lorde/ for he hath done
excellentlye/ and that is knowen thorow ou=
te all the worlde. Crye and showte thou in=
habiter of Sion/ for great amonge you is the
holye of Israel.

Isaiah chapter 12

• SIR WINSTON • • CHURCHILL • • AND THE SECOND • • WORLD WAR •

WHEN the First World War ended in 1918 people spoke as though this was the war that was to end all wars. How far from the truth this was. Wars sadly seem to have been all too frequent of late, due to the greed of those who hold power and who ruthlessly wield it.

When war broke out in our country in 1939 we were very ill equipped to face the hostilities of the battles that lay ahead. In God's mercy and providence a man was raised up to help us in a time of great need. This man was Sir Winston Churchill, who as a gifted statesman was aware of our plight and

rallied the support of the nation, instilling purpose and determination into the hearts of the people. In one of his well known speeches he said: "We shall not flag or fail. We shall go on to the end, we shall fight in France, we shall fight on the seas and oceans, we shall fight with growing confidence and growing strength in the air. We shall defend our island whatever the cost may be. We shall fight on the beaches, we shall fight on the landing grounds, we shall fight in the fields and in the streets, we shall fight in the hills. We shall never surrender. . . ."

Although many lost their lives in the war and there were children who said goodbye to their fathers who never saw them again, many stories have been told of how God was gracious to grant us the victory ultimately. Although we had comparatively few fighter aircraft, at one point Hitler seemed overwhelmed by the success that was afforded to our Spitfire and Hurricane pilots in particular. It is good that each November on Remembrance Day we especially return thanks to God for His mercy to our land and consider those who manifested courage and bravery in a nation where we have been so signally favoured of the LORD.

• The Second World War •

Though now in England for some time
We have from war been free,
We should remember how our land
Much conflict once did see:
For in the last great war much grief
Beset our troubled land,
And lives were lost as brave men sought
For Britain's rights to stand.

And Adolf Hitler for five years,
With hostile power sought
To take away our liberty,
When we with vigour fought
To use the weapons that we had,
Though we were unprepared,
For armaments our enemies used,
And hearts and lives were scarred.

But at a time when many here
Were sad amidst this war,
God in His mercy Churchill used,
Who with much wisdom saw
How all within this land must seek
To break this hostile power,
And many prayed whilst battles raged
At such a trying hour.

And God in mercy answered prayer,
Though casualties there were,
For our small fighters, though but few,
Our enemies now saw,
Were not to be thought lightly of,
As bombers they shot down,
And Hitler's armies realised
We did not fight alone.

Then when in mercy God us gave
The victory o'er our foe,
Sir Winston Churchill and his aids
Immediately did show,
Whilst at St. Margaret's Church, their thanks
For answers to our prayer,
And hearts were cheered and so relieved
They could these tidings share.

• THE •
• PILGRIM FATHERS •

IT was in the year 1620 that a valiant band of men, women and children left Plymouth in a small sailing ship of 180 tons, to set sail for America on a voyage that took two months and thirteen days. The ship, called "The Mayflower", had no cabin accommodation and the occupants faced dangers and discomfort such as can now be hardly imagined! At one point the Captain wanted to turn back, but they manifested great bravery and asked him to sail on because they so much wanted to worship God in a simple way without the forms and ceremonies of man's devising. When they landed they were a great distance north of their original intended landing point and faced awful hardships from the severe winter weather. Though many of them died from exposure, God appeared for them in many ways and they laid the foundation of a new and mighty nation.

• *The Pilgrim Fathers* •

In days when travel overseas
Was dangerous and slow,
The Pilgrim Fathers set to sea,
For they desired to know
A way whereby they could serve God
And more live to His praise;
So for America they sailed,
Though travelling many days.

And oh what trials and problems they
Did meet upon the way,
Yet God in mercy kept them safe,
Though storms them sought to slay.

And then at length their eyes beheld
The land where they could now
Their labours follow, whilst they sought
Unto God praise to show.

So as we think of those who sailed
On that "Mayflower" of old,
We can be thankful that a state
Through them thus did unfold;
And through these early settlers, who
Sought God, as they did plan
To venture forth, a powerful land
And nation thus began.

Meditations

• *Meditation 1* •

My times are in Thy hand.
Psalm 31:15

WHEN the Psalmist uttered these words he appeared to have been suffering some distress in soul and spirit. He speaks in the Psalm of nets which his enemies had laid for him and mentions troubles he had because of his iniquity. In the midst of this we find him encouraging himself in the LORD his God. He reassures himself concerning God's providence and protection, which had come to him in a strong city, and by looking back, seems to gain strength to go forward. Surely there are some lessons here for me. My way at the moment might be somewhat unclear. Uncertainties and disappointments may vex my spirit. If I look back, though, can I honestly say that I have ever been left desolate? No, certainly not, for sometimes severe trials have for me been made the means whereby blessings abundant have become my portion. Need I fear then as I go on? No, if I am fearful it is only because my faith is not in exercise, for God certainly will not fail His people. Oh for a stronger faith, then, so that I might trust my God more even if I cannot trace His purposes.

• *Meditation 2* •

Blessed are the eyes which see the things that ye see.

Luke 10:23

AND what, may I ask, are the things that the disciples saw which made them blessed? What was it that made them rich and Who gave them such wonderful perception? They were blessed, surely, because they saw themselves to be sinful men and had been enlightened concerning the fact that Christ alone could save them from their sin. Their lives were enriched because they could commune with the very One who the prophets looked forward to by faith, Who was to become the fulfilment of the most wonderful promises of God. God grant me true faith, that I might know the joy of these things, and be kept from only seeing with natural eyes as, alas, Judas Iscariot did. Also, may I know the Holy Spirit so deepening my sense of these unseen things that I might know even more joy than the disciples of old.

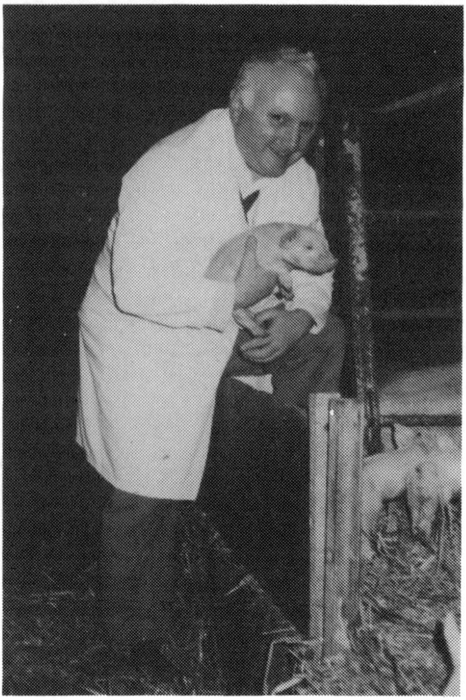

• *Meditation 3* •

And Abraham said, My son, God will provide Himself a lamb for a burnt offering.

Genesis 22:8

THESE words were spoken at a time when Abraham was passing through one of the greatest trials of his life. He had been promised a son and had waited years for this promise to be fulfilled. Now it seems God is going to require such a strange thing of Abraham, for here he is being told to slay his son. But did he disobey, feeling that God must have surely got things wrong this time? No, he meekly goes out to prepare to obey God's command, knowing in his heart that the ways of Jehovah are still to be followed, even if they cannot be understood. And when that ram was provided, what joy must have filled his heart. It might seem to some to be a foolish course to take. Yet if God be in it, He is able to furnish a table in the wilderness and make the rough places smooth. Oh for a stronger faith, then, to trust and not to be afraid — for whate'er lies ahead, God is still the One well able to provide.

• *Meditation 4* •

Things which are despised, hath God chosen.
1 Corinthians 1:28

HOW different are God's ways to my ways. What a contrast there is between the general opinion of men and the sovereign purposes of God. If, however, God has given to me a small portion of His Spirit, so that I have certain mysteries made clearer to me, how thankful ought I to be. Not only should I be thankful, but humility should be more evident in my life. I only know some of my sins, failings and weaknesses: yet God in His goodness has graciously chosen me to be His, secured for me eternal life through the substitutionary work of the Lord Jesus, and given me a purpose in life. May such condescension constrain me to live in such a way as befits my calling. LORD, as I am made to realise Thy ways do far surpass the wisdom of the greatest of men, may I observe Thy wonders, rejoicing in them, knowing how much better it is to trust in Thee than to put confidence in men.

• *Meditation 5* •

For if Abraham were justified by works, he hath whereof to glory; but not before God.
Romans 4:2

ONE of the hallmarks of the true Christian is that he does not speak of what he has done for God, but rather what God has done for him. When many are speaking of their achievements and good life, what is the subject upon which I desire to dwell? Well, since by God's grace I know that my efforts in the matter of attainment are all useless, my theme will be concerning His plan of salvation. I will glory in the fact that because my sins were laid upon the Saviour, when He suffered on the cross, His righteousness has been made over to my account. I will rejoice in the fact that the work of the Lord Jesus was a completed work and nothing can be added to that. LORD, make me aware that whatever I do of myself is but as filthy rags in Thy sight, and grant me the gift of faith to look to the Lord Jesus alone, Who can take away my sin and give me cause to rejoice before Him.

• Meditation 6 •

Verily I say unto you, Whosoever shall not receive the kingdom of God as a little child, he shall not enter therein.

Mark 10:15

WHAT similarities there are between the behaviour of a child and the attitudes of a Christian. In what way should I manifest a childlike spirit? Surely first of all a child is well aware of its own weakness and need of protection by its parents. Then I must remember that unless I have seen myself as a weak creature, unable to do anything of myself to procure favour or protection from God when His judgments are prounounced, then there is no hope for me. Also, a child is one who, if blessed with good parents, is not anxious about what the morrow may bring, or whether there will be provision for the way. No, the child is happy to leave such matters in the hands of the parents. Then ought not I to seek that faith which will enable me to leave all my affairs in the hands of a wise God who has promised that He will not leave nor forsake His people? LORD, give me a childlike faith that will make me an inheritor of Thy kingdom.

• Meditation 7 •

Cause me to hear Thy lovingkindness in the morning; for in Thee do I trust: cause me to know the way wherein I should walk; for I lift up my soul unto Thee.

Psalm 143:8

SOMETHING which makes the Psalms so precious to me is the way in which one can read of the conflict and concerns that men of a bygone age experienced and see how they unburdened their hearts in prayer to God. In this verse we can detect a quiet confidence in the providence of the LORD and see a prayer for guidance along the path of life. Surely if those men who penned these Psalms proved God's faithfulness amidst dangers and distresses in their generation, I too may look up by faith to the One who changeth not, and prove the lovingkindness of God in many remarkable ways.

• Meditation 8 •

But the salvation of the righteous is of the LORD: He is their strength in the time of trouble.

Psalm 37:39

TROUBLE is surely something which comes to all mankind from time to time. A fallen world, where there is much imperfection, means that inevitably distress of many different kinds is never far away from any one of us. Surely it is an evidence of God's mercy when we are kept from many evils that so easily could befall us. For the Christian, his first awareness of deliverance from trouble must surely be when he is made to see that without God's grace, his soul is deserving of nothing but everlasting trouble. Yet as he goes on he can continually testify that whilst problems and trials may beset him, in the midst of them there are evidences of a tender heavenly Father's care. What peace then it is possible to know, even in the midst of a storm.

SLOE
FARM

• Meditation 9 •

Though the LORD be high, yet hath He respect unto the lowly: but the proud He knoweth afar off.

Psalm 138:6

IF humility is something which the LORD delighteth in, how important then it is for me to cultivate a meek and lowly attitude before Him. By realising how great my God is, and how unworthy I am, I will be better enabled to show reverence towards God whilst worshipping Him with His people, and will be helped to trace His tender mercies as they unfold day by day. The LORD abhorreth pride of heart and proud looks: may it not be my portion to be known afar off, because of these things being evident in my heart. Rather may I through a right attitude of heart know my LORD affording me true blessing.

• Meditation 10 •

Thy God hath commanded thy strength: strengthen, O God, that which Thou hast wrought for us.

Psalm 68:28

SOMETIMES we speak about it being a mercy that men are limited in their strength and abilities. When evil rulers boast about their efforts and speak about what they are going to do, surely it's good to remember they can only go as far as they are allowed. In a Christian way though, how thankful we ought to be if we've been made to see that, whereas we thought we were strong in our own righteousness and good works, yet these will not stand the test on the day of judgment. Then we will seek that righteousness which Christ alone can work in us, and we will seek grace that we might manifest outwardly what has taken place inwardly. Work, O God, in my heart that my testimony might be strong in the LORD of hosts.

• Meditation 11 •

Bless the LORD, O my soul, and forget not all His benefits.

Psalm 103:2

THE Psalmist had a deep desire to give thanks unto God for all His mercies. Though he received benefits he desired to look beyond them up to the great Benefactor. David reminds me through this verse to be more aware of God's goodness, so that I might bring praise unto the Most High. I am surrounded by so many who have no desire to ascribe honour unto God for all His goodness. Such people can easily influence me and make me less aware of how dependent I am on the LORD. Therefore, may I rather seek daily to observe God's kindness in all His providences, ever being aware of what a difference there is between what I receive and what I really deserve.

• *Meditation 12* •

As for man, his days are as grass: as a flower of the field, so he flourisheth. For the wind passeth over it, and it is gone; and the place thereof shall know it no more. But the mercy of the LORD is from everlasting to everlasting upon them that fear Him, and His righteousness unto children's children. . . .

Psalm 103:15-17

WITH a few moments to spare the other day, I went for a walk in some young orchards where the bird song sounded so pleasant and the fragrance after a recent shower seemed to add even further to the tranquillity of the place. It was early spring; the blossom made one adore the handiwork of a great Creator and the grass carpeted with wild flowers made one feel it would be good to stay here for some time. Meditating for a while, my mind went to the verse that states so clearly that all natural beauty will soon perish. I remembered that one thing that lasts for ever is my never-dying soul. I called to mind the Scriptures that mention the unchangeableness of the Word of God and considered that though natural wonders be so pleasant, yet how much more wonderful it is to know the God Who made these things, and experience the pardon of all one's transgressions through a living relationship with Christ — a relationship which brings one abundant riches. Oh that I might be more humbly thankful for such grace, that I might more deeply prove the reality of these riches day by day.

• Meditation 13 •

My foot standeth in an even place: in the congregations will I bless the LORD.

Psalm 26:12

HOW blessed I am if this testimony is mine. What a privilege to know the One through whom alone I can stand! The world is a very uncertain place and so many things can happen which cause grief and sadness, but how wonderful through the LORD's goodness to be placed on a firm foundation. The Psalmist in this passage speaks of trusting the LORD, of redemption, of mercy and of wondrous works; and do not these refer to a wonderful salvation? Surely if he could know peace and blessedness — although not witnessing the actual work of the Saviour, but by faith looking forward to it — may not I greatly rejoice in the completion of the plan of salvation, that souls might stand in a secure place? Then indeed will I be able to bless the LORD amongst the congregations of His people. LORD, make me aware that I am only safe when trusting in Thee, and teach me to walk humbly that my feet may be kept safe in an even place.

• Meditation 14 •

The fear of the LORD tendeth to life: and he that hath it shall abide satisfied; he shall not be visited with evil.

Proverbs 19:23

WHAT a blessed life is the Christian life! What security, yea what wonderful resources a Christian has at his disposal! I am reminded, though, that the Scripture says, "according to your faith be it unto you". Therefore, how I need to pray that I will ever be given grace to walk in the fear of the LORD, that I might know that contentment which is rarely seen in these days, even amongst God's people. Now then, if I do know anything of walking in the fear of God, how wonderful to have the assurance that although trials will come, yet the LORD will take the evil of the sting out of them. So may I go onward seeking to know more of that abundant life which the Saviour promised, manifesting peace and tranquillity, when so many are living solely to get more and more, with no real purpose in life. LORD, teach me to walk in Thy fear all the day long, that I may abide sweetly satisfied; and by Thy grace may I triumph in all the vicissitudes of life.

Poems and Pieces for Children

• *For Young People* •

When blessed with youth upon our side
And thinking we may need no guide
To help us on our earthly way,
It's good to pause, and ask, and say,
May I one day the fact regret
That I the Bible did forget,
Which warned me that I have a heart
So prone from right ways to depart?
So therefore I do stand in need
Of help that I might thus be led
In ways whereby I'll be kept free
From sins that grievous to God be.
So may I wisdom seek and prove
The love of One who, though above,
Can be a Saviour unto me,
A Friend from sin to set me free,
As One who can true life impart
And make me happy in my heart.

• THE ORPHAN LAMB •

IT was about four o'clock one October morning. I had been sleeping well, but was awakened by the sound of a wind such as I had never heard in my life before. From the rooftop of my house tiles were being blown about and seemed to make a most frightening noise as they came crashing down on the path below.

For several moments my wife (who had already been awake for some time) and I just laid and listened. We wondered whatever the scene would reveal when light came in the morning. I became very concerned about the animals outside. Would any of them have suffered injury or have been killed? All of a sudden I was really troubled by thoughts about our orphan lamb that had recently joined the small flock grazing around our orchard. Poor Freckles, I thought. Suddenly I felt I must go and rescue him from the orchard. Before my wife could hold me back I had slipped on an old coat. I rushed downstairs, slipped on my boots, and now nothing could stop me from the mission in hand. Once outside I found it a terrible battle to run to the orchard just a hundred yards or so away. Tiles were being blown down and branches were hurtling along at great speed. I could hardly move along. I just prayed that I'd be able to rescue our pet lamb. Somehow I reached the small paddock, and staggered almost like a drunken man over the gate; opening the gate was impossible. I realised I was in the midst of great danger amidst trees that were being uprooted because they could offer little resistance to such a powerful force as was overthrowing them. In the half-light it seemed a most awesome task to now find Freckles and rescue him from such a terrible scene. I must have been helped, because in no time I had him securely in my arms and found myself struggling against great odds to carry him to a less dangerous place. It was only a few moments after we had reached a place of comparative shelter that there was a great thud as two large fir trees fell helplessly to the ground where I had just been. If they had fallen a few moments earlier I would almost without doubt have been killed. How thankful I felt for such protection as God in His mercy had afforded me.

Reflecting upon this incident of some years back still makes me aware of what great kindness God did show to me. I actually risked my life to save a little orphan lamb. How much more wonderful I find it, though, to think about my precious Saviour, even the LORD JESUS. He didn't just risk His life to save His people from their sins, He actually **gave** His life up to a very cruel death on a cross, when He was punished for their sins. He suffered hell when His Father's face was turned against Him, so that those who see their need of forgiveness and pardon, might be delivered from the awfulness of being left for ever suffering from the wrath of God that must be poured out upon those who die unrepentant. I find it fills me with a sense of great relief to know that when the awful hurricane of God's displeasure against sin must shortly be revealed, I'll be safe in that day. I wonder, are you prepared for that solemn day?

• A JCB •

One tractor well known to us all,
On farms and in towns too,
Is a JCB digger that
So many jobs can do.
And grand it is to see one used
Down on some building site,
Where levers are both pushed and pulled
To lay things out just right.

Then as hydraulics operate
For footings 'neath the soil
To be prepared, so work is done
Through rams controlled by oil;
And what a great invention 'twas
When man the way could see,
Tasks to perform and time to save,
With the first JCB.

For with the bucket at the front
A lorry it can load,
And products such as bales and corn
Are lifted ere they're towed.
And if their history we could trace
Of some things that we eat,
The JCB could tell us how
It worked to bring us meat.

Yes, for this grand machine we ought
Most thankful then to be,
And when in factories they are made
By men whose skills you see,
We should to God give gratitude
That in a land we live,
With JCBs and drivers who
Great service to us give.

• Farm Safety •

If children would from grief be free,
When farms and animals they see,
They would do well my words to heed,
For in these days there is great need
To take great care down at the farm,
Where some, alas, have come to harm.
It is important that you know,
That near machines you should not go,
Which though they're guarded, still could be
The means to hurt both you and me.

And other hazards here there be,
Besides those on machinery,
For farmers lots of straw require,
Which is susceptible to fire.
What caution therefore you must take,
Lest through your folly you should make
A fire break out and cause distress,
And then to wrongful ways confess.
How vital is it then to show
Consideration as you go.

Of something else you should take heed:
For farmers have continual need
Of ample electricity;
So wires in farmyards there must be.
Therefore remember, never throw
Such things as stones where powerlines go;
And should you see a lorry tip
Near cables, then with tongue and lip
That driver warn to keep well clear
Of unseen danger in the air.

So from these things I trust you see
That farms can dangerous places be,
And when due care has not been shown,
Some grievous accidents have known:
So listen then to what I say
And to all warnings good heed pay,
Then safe you'll be and pleasure know
As you in farming knowledge grow
And help to others then impart
Through things impressed upon your heart.

· THE TEN ·
· COMMANDMENTS ·

THE Ten Commandments can be divided into two sections; the first four concern our relationship to God, and the last six are to do with our relationship to our fellow men. Nobody has ever kept all of the Commandments perfectly (except for the LORD JESUS, of course) and the reason for this is because we are all born into this world as sinners and are all wrong in our hearts. In fact, just by being angry in our heart towards another in a wrong way, is a sin in God's sight. The Commandments were not given to be the means of our salvation, but rather they show us how we have all sinned and come short of the glory of God, and how we stand in need of the Saviour, even the LORD JESUS CHRIST, to be our substitute. If we are aware of our failure and sin then we will seek mercy from God who has promised that those who confess and forsake their sin will have Christ's righteousness made over to them, through faith that is the gift of God. Then as we are made aware of what debtors we are to God's mercy we will desire to do those things that please Him, although continually needing pardon, because none of us can ever attain to perfection in this life.

Of the LORD JESUS we read in 1 Peter 2:24: "Who His own self bare our sins in His own body on the tree, that we, being dead to sins, should live unto righteousness: by whose stripes ye were healed."

• God's Commandments •

When Moses was raised up of God,
So many years ago,
The LORD revealed to man through him
Some laws we ought to know;
And graven on two stones were given
Commandments very clear,
About our conduct on this earth,
Where we should God's laws hear.

These laws remind us we should not
Take God's great Name in vain,
And should not worship images
Carved out by skilful men.
Then every week we should observe
One day for rest, that we
Might bear in mind we've souls as well,
Which pardoned need to be.

Then to our parents, God has said,
That honour should be shown,
And He has promised graciously
That He will then make known
Long life to those who here obey
This law within their home,
Because God's promised mercy shall
With this commandment come.

Then we are told it's wrong to kill,
And pure our lives should be,
And all distasteful ways and acts
Should not desire to see;
But thankful be for those we love
And faithful be to them,
That in our ways God's Word will not
Our doings here condemn.

That stealing is to God a sin
He has to us made clear,
Then how we need to take much care —
Yet all, alas, I fear
Have failed God here at certain times,
Though this sin think we small:
Yet break we one — then in God's eyes
We have them broken all.

False witnessing, God's Word makes clear,
Is wrong in every way;
By coveting our neighbour's goods
His laws we disobey.
Yet all our hearts are so corrupt
And wrong before the LORD,
For all fall short of that made clear
Within His holy Word.

But though God's laws we all transgress
And fail Him day by day,
How wonderful to know Christ came
To show to us the way —
To pardon know from the Most High,
When He for us became
Our Saviour, who removed our guilt —
All glory to His Name.

So out of love and gratitude,
For such great love displayed,
In God's laws we should then delight,
If we have now been made
Pure in God's sight, from all our sin,
And now set fair for Heaven —
Then praise to God for matchless grace
Shall evermore be given.

· THE LOST BULL ·

WHEN I was eighteen and had recently started working for my Dad on our family farm, I decided I'd very much like to gain some experience in dairy farming. On our own farm we really specialised in producing arable crops, such as wheat, barley and sugarbeet, and did not have any grassland at all. My minister told me of a farm on an island on the west of Scotland with dairy cattle where he said I'd be welcome to stay for a while. He very kindly made arrangements for me to go and stay there for a fortnight in June 1970. Now up to that point in my life I'd never really travelled very far and the thought of travelling 400 miles or so to a place and people that I had never met before, filled me with a sense of nervous excitement. One evening, though, with my case packed, I set off for the Isle of Arran by train. I now faced a fifteen hour journey, travelling via Peterborough, up the eastern side of our country towards Edinburgh and then westwards to Glasgow, where I would have to change trains. My travelling time would have been reduced if I'd travelled via London, but I didn't want to pay £15 for a ticket when a £12 one would take me to the same place. In any case, the travelling was for me part of the holiday, so a longer journey didn't bother me.

On arriving in Glasgow I faced a two-hour wait for another connection and passed the time munching an apple or two. It was here I first heard people speaking in real Scottish accents and this made me wonder if I'd ever be able to interpret what the people on the remote island of Arran would say to me! Quickly the time passed though and I found myself on a train bound for the port of Ardrossan where I could catch the ferry to Arran. The journey across the water took fifty minutes and as the views of the mountains and hills of Arran came into view with the cattle contentedly grazing, I thought of the verse that says, "For every beast of the forest is mine, and the cattle upon a thousand hills" (Psalm 50:10).

The main port of Arran is called Brodick and here a well-worn bus took me across one of the two roads that cross the island to Balmichael Farm, where I was to stay with Mr. Colin Currie. Mr. Currie had inherited the farm from his father and it was one of the larger farms of Arran. Here there was much grassland which supported a beautiful herd of Ayrshire cows kept for milk production. On a bleak hill towards the sea some hardy Blue Greys were kept as suckler cows for rearing calves and with them grazed a large Hereford bull. There were also sheep on the farm.

I was soon made to feel very much at home on the farm. Mrs. Currie cooked excellent food and I became part of a team working with Michael and Ronald, who were employees here. I started work very early in the morning and after helping with the milking and then enjoying a good breakfast joined Michael for a long walk to check the animals upon the hill. This took us up to coffee time. One day, whilst making our daily check on things, we found to our dismay that the large Hereford bull had broken through a weak part of the fence and, although all the cows were still grazing, he appeared to have fled over the hills and gone far away. We spent some time looking around and listening and then felt we should report back to Balmichael so that neighbours could be alerted.

Now on Arran there is a good atmosphere between farming folk and several offered to help to look for the lost bull. However, in spite of helpful willing hands, two days actually passed before we found the animal in question. As one who was so much enjoying the beautiful scenery of Arran, two days spent hunting high and low passed blissfully away for me, although I was concerned about the damage this animal might cause. When he was actually tracked down, he was found at the bottom of a deep ditch with his head well and truly stuck between the trunks of two large trees. He did not appear to have broken any bones and mercifully the ditch only contained about two feet of water.

As word passed round to those involved in this little adventure that the much sought for animal was now found, the next question was, How would we free the naughty fellow? Someone suggested calling in the slaughtermen and having him cut up for the table, but as Mr. Currie had paid around £800 for him, this suggestion did not go down very well. It was therefore decided that a large chain saw must be sought that one of the trees could be cut down. One of the farmers on the island said that he would loan his saw for this operation. It was actually my job to collect a tractor from the farm and a long rope, so that we could ensure that as the tree was almost ready to fall it would come away from the bull to prevent injury. As I sat on the tractor with the rope held taut and my foot feathering the clutch ready to move forward at first command, I prayed much that this operation would be successful. After several minutes cutting, which seemed to last an age, the drone of the chain saw suddenly stopped and someone shouted, "Pull, Raymond", and this large tree came crashing to the ground. Immediately I switched off the tractor and anxiously ran back to see if the bull was now able to free itself. Already Michael and Ronald were encouraging the bull to climb out by gently pulling on its halter. We were all so thankful and amazed to find that still it had the strength to haul itself out, though as its back feet left the ditch it did stagger a

little. Somewhat ironically as it paused for breath, it seemed to stare at the chain saw almost with an expression of appreciation. "That was your saviour, old boy," Michael called out, as we stood now all very relieved at the end of two days of anxious suspense.

As I started to help clear up the tackle and take it back to the farm I thought about what a wonderful Saviour the LORD JESUS is. Surely as human beings we all have broken out, not from a paddock, but from the restrictions that God first of all put upon our first parents, Adam and Eve. As a result we have brought great distress upon ourselves through sin, and if left to ourselves we can never escape the awful consequences of displeasing God and should be left to perish eternally. How amazing, though, that the LORD JESUS saw our plight and came to earth to take a body like our own, though without sin, and then die and be punished for the sins of those who trust in Him. As I thought about that bull, now safe and out of danger because of a chain saw that became its deliverer, I couldn't but be amazed at such a wonderful heavenly Saviour I have, who has dealt with all the consequences of all my wrongdoing. I wonder is JESUS CHRIST your Saviour too?

• A SPECIAL •
• CAR RADIO •

ON being invited on one occasion to travel with a friend to a meeting, a journey which involved passing through lovely scenery, I gladly accepted the invitation. Because my friend's car was quite up-to-date with various gadgets and devices, I was pleased to have the opportunity to find out a bit more about it and I thought this would make the trip even more interesting. We hadn't travelled very far before we heard pips coming over the radio and then immediately we picked up some travel news from the radio station of the county towards which we were travelling. I was told that because the radio was an advanced computerised model, then all travel reports from some distance ahead would be picked up. Sure enough it wasn't long before a travel news flash was broadcast from a county even further afield. My friend told me of the way in which in the course of his work he is helped to avoid many traffic jams and dangerous areas through travel items picked up with the help of advanced technology. He told me of the way this saves him time and trouble on many occasions.

Reflecting on the subject of being saved from dangers, I began to think of the way in which the Bible too sends out signals and tells us of dangers along the pathway of life. I reminded myself that so often I bring myself into difficulties because I don't heed the warnings given, probably because I'm not tuned into the signal being broadcast. At one point during the travel news being picked up on my friend's radio, some sport's news was coming over too, and this was because of some error concerning the transmission.

I thought of the way in which the Bible is never in error, yet so often I can overlook the instruction through a breakdown in my communications with the LORD. I did feel so thankful, though, after reflecting on these things, because although I fail the LORD so often and bring myself into trouble and others too, yet I know that though hell will be the place where people go who reject God's Word, this will never be my lot. By God's grace I have been made to see my need of a Saviour who can deliver me from that terrible place. Therefore I know that though I may fail and fall, yet ultimately I will end my journey in Heaven. Now I know this is not because I deserve to, but because unworthy though I be, my Saviour has undertaken to take me home on high at the last, and then all the dangers along my journey of life will be for ever at an end.

Poems and Pieces relating to Christian Experience

• *Of Praise to God* •

Oh LORD as we now meet
We join to bless Thy Name,
Who art the Most High God,
Eternally the same.
Whilst we have hearts that are unclean
And punished should be for our sin:

Yet praise we bring to Thee,
For Christ, who died to save,
When He atonement made
For many, as He gave
His life that sinners so unclean
Might pardoned be for all their sin.

Then thankful we now are
For such a Substitute,
And may we in our lives
To Thy praise bring forth fruit,
With hearts renewed — no more unclean —
As those who now detest all sin.

Then soon that day will come
When we shall fail no more,
But in the "Glory Land"
Our Saviour we'll adore
As those redeemed — no more unclean —
But free for ever from all sin.

• The Precious Bible •

In England, oh how blessed we are
To have the Word of God!
For light it gives, as those well knew
Who for it shed their blood.

No other book can help afford
For man's most pressing need,
And souls in darkness here may learn
From guilt how to be freed.

There good instruction we are given
To order well our lives,
And more than that, it tells of hope
One can have when one dies.

When we did keep God's laws we knew
More blessing in our land —
But now we've turned aside, we see
The judgments of His hand.

But while the Bible still we have,
We know God can us bless,
And through the preaching of His Word
Men yet their sins confess.

And blessing rich again we'd know,
As known in former days,
If men would to the Bible turn
And love its wondrous ways.

• God's Amazing Mercy •

LORD Thy mercy fills the earth —
This is seen in every birth;
Those with eyes may surely tell,
How God doeth all things well.

When we look into the sky,
There we see Thy majesty;
From the soil, where seeds we sow,
Plants spring forth Thy power to show.

What amazing mercy too
Do we see in trees that grow:
For these things that we behold,
We would have Thy Name extolled.

Yet for work our souls to save,
By the Saviour, when He gave
All He had, that we might be
Cleansed and saved eternally.

Praise, eternal praise is Thine,
Here Thy brightest glories shine;
Fallen man may speak and tell,
Of a love that saves from hell.

Thus, great God, our thanks we bring,
Of Thy grace and care we'd sing,
While on earth — and then above
Thee we'll praise for all Thy love.

• About Assurance •

How blessed am I, if I with Paul
Can say I know Christ died
To be my Saviour from my sin
When He was crucified;
And as His Spirit in my heart
Persuades me of His love,
How wonderful to rest assured
I'm loved by One above.

So whilst around me there are those
That Christ-rejectors be,
Within my soul I'm safe, and will
To all eternity
Extol a Saviour who His all
For those He loved did give,
That they in Heaven great bliss might know
And there for ever live.

• WHY I ENJOY •
• BEING A FARMER •

. . . BUT EVEN MORE ENJOY BEING A CHRISTIAN

THE reasons why I enjoy being a farmer are manifold, but to be a Christian brings far more joys than a rich king ruling a great empire — yet alas without knowing God — could ever know. When one is a farmer, many opportunities are given of witnessing God's mighty acts of creation, such as the recurring seasons which pass year by year. A farmer is often privileged in being able to enjoy lovely open spaces and fascinating cloud patterns passing overhead, causing one to wonder, adore and give praise. Although at certain seasons I need to be out in the middle of a cold crisp night, yet even then I can pause for an occasional moment, look up and behold a myriad of stars and recall to mind the Scripture which declares: "He telleth the number of the stars; He calleth them all by their names" (Psalm 147:4). Although such thoughts fill one with a sense of awe, yet in one's innermost being there can be experienced great peace in one's soul, for the great Creator who controls the balancing of all the planets in the universe has become the Friend of unworthy sinners purchased through the pardoning work of the LORD JESUS when He died upon the cross.

As one is able to enjoy seeing crops grow and develop, then bring forth fruit in their season, it is good to be able to contemplate that God is a God of order, yet He also created a diversity of colours. The old adage says that "the grass is always greener on the other side", but when God visits the heart and makes all things new, one can enjoy with fresh eyesight the sun arise upon the undulating countryside, admire the woods in the distance, hear the birds chanting praise to Him who made them, and then in the evening see different colours with varying shades that were not evident in the morning light.

Not only is it good to behold God's splendour in plants, trees, changing skies and seasons, but also in the livestock of a mixed farm one is often able to stand back and admire, for instance, the lovely pattern of creamy white and golden brown colours adorning a young calf. Maybe the calf has a much more attractive coat than its mother. Perhaps someone may say that it must be due to genetics or the throwback of a previous generation — yet the true reason is that God ordered it so, since He made all things and for His pleasure they were and are created (Revelation 4:11).

As it is sometimes my joy to see a new born lamb come into the world, one has to praise God for such beautiful creatures and the miracle of birth — and miracle it is, since man with all his technology cannot even create a blade of grass. But as one sees a lamb stagger to its feet, scarcely having the strength so to do (perhaps needing the ewe to lick its body to stimulate the heart and vitalise the nerves), one can consider the greater joy in one's heart when God makes a man a Christian, with new motives, new aspirations, causing him to bring forth fruit unto righteousness. And when God starts the work He will perform it unto the day of Jesus Christ (Philippians 1:6). The life of that new lamb is uncertain, very uncertain; maybe a hungry fox is lurking not far away and soon, if there is no awareness of that danger, the lamb will be no more. If it survives to be no longer in danger of foxes, yet there are diseases and parasites that could strike at any time. How uncertain, then, is the life of a lamb, and even should it escape all these things unscathed, yet ere long it will meet up with the knife of the ruthless butcher — and rightly so, since God has said: "Every creature of God is good, and nothing to be refused, if it be received with thanksgiving" (1 Timothy 4:4). How different it is, though, with the life of the Christian. When God begins a work in a man there is no "maybe" about it. True, a Christian may and does fall into sin, yet God will not allow His child to lie still in sin. Trials may become his lot, he will be made aware of a holy longing and will cry out: "Create in me a clean heart, O God; and renew a right spirit within me" (Psalm 51:10). Then — and only then — will he be able to know, like David of old after committing great sin, that "the LORD . . . hath put away thy sin; thou shalt not die" (2 Samuel 12:13).

Yes, agriculture can be a most interesting and fascinating business to a mind enlightened by the grace and goodness of God . . . but it needs to be said also that it can be a very disheartening and distressing business. Many things can come in and remind us that we are merely created, sinful, human beings; and as such we are very dependent human beings. When the ravages of fire destroy an entire harvest in the barn and a hailstorm dashes all hopes of a plentiful harvest overnight, bringing one perhaps near to bankruptcy, it is a reminder that as reliant creatures upon God's providence we should be humble creatures and continually acknowledge that all our times are in His hands (Psalm 31:15). I have known a disease such as pneumonia take away three young calves in the space of a few hours and gastro-enteritis cause the death of fifty young piglets in one week (and this on a comparatively small farm). What a reminder of how dangerous — yea, sinful — it is to boast in "all the works that my hands have wrought" (Ecclesiastes 2:11).

In farming there is a continual battle with things opposing growth and development. When Adam fell and sinned in the Garden of Eden, soon after God created the world, a curse was pronounced upon the earth. Now instead of man "dressing and keeping it" as it was in the time of man's innocence, there is a continual struggle with thorns and thistles. The earth left to itself will not produce clean crops, there must be cultivation, pesticides and fungicides applied, etc., and man is constantly finding out that as new diseases are counteracted, others are often springing up. Sometimes the reason for this is our greed has upset the balance of God's creation. How sad it is to see that the heart of man is like soil, and left to "free expression", as in our present society, there is wickedness to such an extent that our very rulers are calling good evil, and evil good.

Yes, farming teaches me many things. It makes it clear to me that the LORD "openest His hand, and satisfiest the desire of every living thing" (Psalm 145:16). It teaches me that "the eyes of all wait upon Thee; and Thou givest them their meat in due season". The reason why some have plenty whilst others die is, perhaps, bad distribution and man's greed — yea, my greed.

I enjoy farming because it also shows me the way that God can turn apparent disaster to work for the best. In 1987 we had such a wet autumn that at the time of the closure of the sugar beet factory where we sell our crop, there were still forty tons remaining in the fields. Was this going to be a calamity? We thought so, yet being blessed with a mixed farm it was suggested that our beet could become part of an integrated feeding programme for our animals. The result was that the animals over that period became more prolific with better results all round . . . and to God's name be the praise. Truly God's ways are higher than our ways. This is true if we take a parallel with the Gospel. When the LORD JESUS died on the cross it was, His disciples thought, a disaster. "We trusted," they said, "that it had been He which should have redeemed Israel: and beside all this, today is the third day since these things were done" (Luke 24:21). Little did they know that at that point a most glorious conquest had been achieved. When the LORD JESUS rose from the dead He demonstrated that His suffering was, for those who trust in Him, the means whereby their sins could be atoned for, that they might be free from condemnation and know everlasting life.

Now though I enjoy being a farmer, I trust that I have feebly shown you how much more enjoyable it is to be a Christian and I hope that as long as my brief life lasts I will go on learning a bit more about these things until faith is turned to sight. And then — oh happy thought! — Heaven itself will become for me, a hell-deserving sinner, a place where there are pleasures for evermore.

• *In Defence of the* •
• *Authorised Version* •

In days when versions of God's Word
Are in abundance found,
This makes me sad, for they speak forth
With an uncertain sound;
But I am glad the old A.V.
Today still many love,
For here they sense that "The Most High"
Has spoken from above.

And in this version when they read,
They feel that here's a book
That's different from all other books,
And feel constrained to look
To Christ, who by His Word did show
To lost and ruined men,
We're all corrupt, and to be saved
We must be born again.

With many versions seen today,
Some verses have been changed,
As if to say that modern man
Must have things rearranged;
But when most clear the A.V. speaks
Of Paul and his own good
As "dung" before God: cannot this
Be clearly understood?

Then when one seeks to learn by heart
God's Word and hide it there,
The version easiest to retain,
In tones both sweet and clear,
Is the King James, where one receives
Impressions most divine,
And here God's greatness is revealed
And all His glories shine.

So though today the shops may sell
New versions of God's Word,
The old A.V. remains the one
Which does to me afford
Meat for my soul, to strengthen me
Through all my pilgrim way,
And soon its promises I'll prove
When dawns the eternal day.

• *"Great are Thy* •
• *Tender Mercies"* •

When I look back upon my former days,
Much cause I have, O LORD, Thy Name
to praise:
For oh what mercies I have daily seen,
When in my ways I have so wayward been;
Then what have I in which I then may boast,
Save in the grace which rescued me
when lost?

And as my present days I think upon,
Now still I am aware of mercies shown
And blessed I am to know that all things here
Are working for the best — then need
I fear?
Because whatever state I may be in,
Thy grace, O God, will surely there be seen.

So as I view my days, look where I may —
Today, what's gone, and at my future way —
Glad in my spirit I then ought to be,
As one made safe to all eternity;
And so much glory to Thee may I bring,
By life and lip may I Thy praises sing.

• *God on the Throne* •

When in prosperity,
Days of much bliss I see —
Should I not then think of God on the Throne?

When through adversity,
I may afflicted be,
May I remember God is on the Throne.

When in my land I see,
Matters that grievous be,
Should I not then think of God on the Throne?

When wars so oft take place
And hostile foes men face,
Still may I call to mind God is on the Throne.

When death calls friends away,
May I look up and still pray,
Ever rejoicing that God is on the Throne.

Then when death calls e'en for me,
And I my Saviour will see,
Truly I'll happy be God is on the Throne.

• THE PSALMS •

THOUGH written many years ago, the Psalms have been a great blessing to those who love the LORD for countless generations. There are Psalms of praise and adoration; Psalms which express gratitude to God for His mercy and goodness; Psalms of confession of sin; Psalms of supplication; and Psalms which extol the LORD for His power and majesty. Indeed, the writers of the Psalms can be seen in many different frames of mind as they were divinely inspired to record these words, and at all seasons one can witness them calling upon God. After King David had committed adultery and been made aware of his wickedness, his grief and sorrow for his sin caused him to cry out in true repentance with words that many have since made their own personal prayer. We can read these words of contrition and humility in Psalm 51. Metrical Psalms enable us to praise God with singing and are used frequently both in the public worship of God and at family worship in many homes.

• *The Psalms* •

Though all the writers of God's Word
To me instruction give;
In David's Psalms I love to dwell,
And almost in them live.

For when I'm low and much downcast,
This comfort brings to me;
Even King David felt this way
And found a remedy.

When I some answered prayer have known
And want to praise my LORD;
To certain Psalms I love to turn,
Which help in this afford.

David, I know, God's works enjoyed
And talked much of His grace,
Whilst he his sheep did tend, he knew
The smilings of God's face.

And when his en'mies him pursued
And hardship he did know,
He trusted in the LORD of Hosts,
Triumphing o'er the foe.

He also knew that of himself
He easily could fall;
And grievous sin committed when
On God he did not call.

But true repentance he did show
And blest forgiveness knew,
When God's enriching love to him
Descended like the dew.

Through all the Psalms I feel I can
Know blessing in my soul,
And see how David at all times
His great God did extol.

And oh may I my God thus praise
And meditate and pray;
Then for the Psalms I will be glad
Through all my earthly way.

• THE LORD'S DAY •

A surgeon was once interviewing a man in need of his help. He found that this man had been working seven days a week and had brought trouble upon himself. From a drawer the surgeon took out a Bible and told his patient that he had been disobeying the instructions of the One who had made us. He pointed out how wise and kind God was to appoint one day in the week for us to rest our minds and bodies. The surgeon then opened another drawer and took out a knife, which he said he would now have to use because surgery was required.

A few quotes follow from some well known personalities concerning their views on the Sabbath Day:

SIR ROBERT PEEL
Founder of a regular Police Force in Britain

"I never knew a man escape failure, in either body or mind, who worked seven days a week."

SIR WINSTON CHURCHILL
Former Conservative Prime Minister

"Sunday is a divine and priceless institution, the necessary pause in the national life. It is the birthright of every British subject, our responsibility, privilege and duty to hand on to posterity."

BISHOP J. C. RYLE
First Bishop of Liverpool

"The observance of a Sabbath Day is part of the eternal Law of God. The Sabbath is God's merciful appointment for the common benefit of all mankind."

ERIC H. LIDDELL
Olympic Gold Medallist

"There are many people today who think of those who honour Sundays in the old-fashioned way as kill-joys. They feel that during the years of youth they ought to 'have their fling'. Give me the day of rest, when all that savours of organised games can be put on one side, and all life's joys will be greater because of it. To me personally it is a time of communion and fellowship with God — a time of quiet, in fact, a time of re-creation by fellowship with God. I believe that Sunday as we have had it in the past is one of the greatest helps in a young man's life to keep all that is noblest, truest and best. That is why I say, 'Young person, stand for Sunday, for by losing it you will lose the spirit that it stands for'."

PROFESSOR VERNA WRIGHT
Professor of Rheumatology at Leeds University

"The student should observe a Sabbath rest just as much as the manual labourer. As the student keeps a Sabbath rest day he rests his mind and he honours God. To such God says, 'Them that honour Me I will honour'. We ignore the Sabbath at our peril. We keep it to our inestimable benefit."

"If thou turn away thy foot from the Sabbath, from doing thy pleasure on My holy day; and call the Sabbath a delight, the holy of the LORD, honourable; and shalt honour Him, not doing thine own ways, nor finding thine own pleasure, nor speaking thine own words: then shalt thou delight thyself in the LORD; and I will cause thee to ride upon the high places of the earth, and feed thee with the heritage of Jacob thy father: for the mouth of the LORD hath spoken it" (Isaiah 58:13-14).

• *The Lord's Day* •

LORD for Thy day I would give thanks,
When I can learn of Thee;
When, where the Gospel is made known,
I with Thy saints can be.

When sweet refreshment I can know
Through this Thy holy day,
To strengthen me in mind and heart,
And cheer me on my way.

For in this world so much I find
That dulls my inmost need,
Yet with Thy people I am blest,
As on Thy Word I feed.

So may I value this Thy day,
And blessings through it know,
Which will me help throughout my life,
Whilst I am here below.

• *After a Drought* •

When rain does fall and end a drought
How glad our spirits are,
For water we have prayed so long,
But now we blessing share;
And since these showers come from Thee,
Fruitful to make the land,
'Tis right that praises we show forth
To bless Thy gracious hand.

And as the earth the rain requires
To blossom and bear fruit,
So do our souls have needs as well,
Which only grace can suit:
For without that we dead remain
And impure is the heart;
But if Thy Spirit visits us,
That deadness will depart.

Thus teach us from the need of rain
That greater needs there be,
And visit us and bless our land
With true prosperity:
Then rich we'll be towards the LORD
And fruit that's good we'll bear,
Nor barren will our lives then be
As we Thy praise declare.

• *God my Guide* •

Since God is my guide,
Then why should I be
Perplexed when I'm tried,
Whilst waiting on Thee:
For though I'm unsure
Of the pathway ahead,
God will give me grace
And through Him I'll be led.

His Word He has given
To act as my guide,
To lighten my path
Through teaching applied;
And here from Thy people
Of old may I learn,
Who teach me to trust Thee
And from wrong ways turn.

So strengthen my faith
And help me each day,
Whate'er be my lot,
To trust and to pray:
Then though there be hardship,
Which would lay me low,
Thou wilt through these sorrows
Rich blessings bestow.

• *"Be Ye Thankful"* •

When families round their table meet
To eat their daily bread,
How sad that in these days it's rare
For grace first to be said;
And how displeasing it must be
To God as "The Most High",
When we ungrateful do appear
To His "all-seeing eye".

So may we then more thankful be
When we of food partake,
And seek in all humility,
A habit there to make —
To bow our heads before we eat
And give our Maker praise
For His provision for our needs,
And kindness of His ways.

And once again in this loved land,
In homes may families read
The Bible round their table, that
On God's Word they might feed;
And may young children once again
Be taught there day by day,
And learn of God through Christ, who is
The Life, the Truth, the Way.

So since in England we are blessed
And never short of food,
May we have hearts that thanks express
To One who is so good;
But whilst our bodies are enriched,
Through so much we are given,
Within our souls may we be wise
And seek the Bread from Heaven.

• God our Refuge •

"God is our refuge and our strength" —
Thus does the Scripture read,
And what a promise is here found
For all His people's need.

"God is our refuge and our strength,"
Our fathers once could say,
When in their time they knew distress
And many a trying day.

God as their refuge and their strength
The Israelites once knew,
When Pharoah did them sorely chide
And waters they passed through.

God as his refuge and his strength
The Psalmist surely proved,
When though his foes encamped him round,
He stood firm, nor was moved.

God as his refuge and his strength
Old Abraham enjoyed,
When tried and tested for so long
In God he did confide.

God is our refuge and our strength,
And surely He remains
The hope of those who trust Him still —
Whatever He ordains.

• God's Greatness •

Within this world what works there are
Which do a Maker's power declare;
And these things surely demonstrate
God in His ways is truly great.

By skies and stars one can be told
Of glories which such things unfold,
And clouds which pass do clearly state
God in His ways is truly great.

Since man and beast are daily fed
On meat and grain and rice and bread;
When on the Lord all creatures wait,
God, we must say, is truly great.

As flowers such fragrance do afford
From gardens, when a shower's outpoured,
These things He did alone create —
And surely He is truly great.

When skill to man He does bestow
To benefit this world below:
Such things again do illustrate
God in His ways is truly great.

And since on Him I do rely,
I'll seek the grace He can supply,
Then, as His help I supplicate,
I'll prove my God is truly great.

• "MAD COW DISEASE" •

BOVINE Spongiform Encephalopathy — or B.S.E. — is a disease affecting cattle that came about some years ago. Many believe it was caused by scientists trying to incorporate into feeding stuffs materials which our Creator never intended they should have. This surely demonstrates that if we go against God's ways then trouble is bound to come. Although it may be difficult to cite chapter and verse to prove that cows should not have meat and bonemeal incorporated into their ration, nonetheless it is a fact that the stomach of a cow is different from that of a pig which, as a scavenger, will pick up all sorts of things and naturally eat them. Most farmers are very particular what feeds their animals have, because they want their products to be a good and healthy source of nourishment for all. However, B.S.E., like many other things, has been made to sound much worse because of the tendency of the media to blow things up out of all proportion.

• *Beef and B.S.E.* •

When beef is looked upon as bad,
Through talk of B.S.E.,
I'm glad that I can still enjoy
Good meat, and thankful be.

For my own cattle have been reared
On food that suits them well:
Whilst some misguided farmers feed
Things merchants should not sell.

And though men think they know so much
Concerning a cow's need,
Yet if God's pattern they reject
Then problems come indeed.

So I am glad to hear of some
Now questioning their ways,
And trust that matters, so blown up,
Will fade in a few days.

For beef is good and given by God
To nourish and sustain,
So farmers trust their work and toil
Will not be done in vain.

• *Relating to Snow* •

How lovely in the winter time,
When freshly falls the snow,
To watch the sparkling flakes descend
Upon the earth below.

Then for a while it seems so pure
And pleasant to behold;
Yes, children in it love to play
And do not mind the cold.

Yet when the snow has laid a while
It soon becomes defiled,
And what a picture of how sin
Has hearts and lives now spoiled.

How wonderful, though, is Christ's love,
Who came to deal with sin,
That sinners who repent might know
Their hearts made pure and clean.

Then like the Psalmist they may say,
Their hearts are now more white
Than new-lain snow, and are approved
In God's most holy sight.

So may the snow at winter time
Remind me of that love,
That Christ displayed by suffering so
When He came from above.

And may Christ's righteousness alone
My hope and portion be,
Then soon I'll join that ransomed throng
In bliss without degree.

• *About Contentment* •

When I God's blessings do survey,
Which daily come to me,
Within my heart much shame I feel,
Where hardness there can be.

For though so much I have been given
And loved ones me surround,
Yet sadly I so oft complaim,
Whilst mercies do abound.

So help me LORD to be content,
From murmuring keep me free;
Grant me submission to Thy ways
And true humility.

• *For a Twenty-fifth* • • *Anniversary* •

"Thou shalt remember all the way which the LORD thy God led thee. . . . "

Though time flies by, the seasons pass
And anniversaries come and go,
It's good sometimes to meditate
On what the LORD has brought us through:
For He most surely is the One
Who daily does for us provide,
And we are blessed to know He will
For ever be our strength and guide.

So praise to God we must ascribe,
For those with whom we join today,
Who can look back and testify
They've help known through their
pilgrim way;
For through their marriage they have proved
That God does hear and answer prayer,
And when affliction's been their lot
On Him they sought to cast their care.

So for their faithfulness and love
We would to One above give praise,
And trust that through days yet to come
God will them bless in wondrous ways;
And we do pray their families too,
Through blessed experience all may say:
"God has been good — immensely good,
And Him we'll trust and will obey."

• *The Burden of Sin* •

When Christians in their pathway find
That sin does plague them so,
And through their weakness often fail
And grief of heart they know:
What comfort they may prove, as in
The Scriptures they confide,
And from them learn their sins are cleansed,
Because the Saviour died.

Thus though aware of wrong within,
They know that in God's sight
They're counted pure, and justified
With hearts that now are white:
And their desire is for more grace,
That they may day by day,
O'ercome their weakness and God please
And His precepts obey.

So for enabling they do pray
To live unto God's praise,
And every day they plead for help
To keep them from ill ways;
And though they know still in their hearts
There is so much that's wrong,
Ere long for them all will be changed
And for that day they long.

• *God's Providence* •

Great God, Who dost Thy servants guide,
And lead them day by day,
How good to trace Thy providence
At work along the way.

For oftentimes I can behold
An answer to a prayer:
Oh may this teach me at all times
On Thee to cast my care.

For sometimes disappointments come
And trials which vex my mind,
But these afflictions are ordained
By One who is so kind.

Now though Thy ways mysterious be,
Yet when Thy saints look back,
They'll see Thy hand in wisdom worked
And skill it did not lack.

So may Thy people trust Thee more
And not so fearful be;
Commit their ways into Thy hands
In true humility.

• *Things Eternal* •

In days when all around there are
Great changes that I see,
Help me to value from Thy Word
Things which eternal be.

When worldly goods the heart does crave,
Unhelpful unto me,
May I esteem as greater worth
Things which eternal be.

When war and strife affect our land
With some calamity,
True peace afford whilst I behold
Things which eternal be.

When various trials and grief I know
And much perplexity,
Joy may I know in things divine —
Things which eternal be.

And when disease with pain does come
To cause adversity,
Strength may I know, because I view
Things which eternal be.

Then when it is my time to die,
I'll face that joyfully,
Because my soul was taught by grace
Things which eternal be.

Poems as Prayers

• For Greater Faith •

Oh teach me LORD to trust Thee more,
To wait on Thee from hour to hour,
And not to burden my own mind
With anxious cares of every kind.

And may I from the Scriptures learn
To leave to Thee all my concern
In ways and matters, then I'll know
Of peace the world cannot bestow.

So keep me then from sinful ways
And make my life show forth Thy praise;
To do Thy will may I delight
And shun those things wrong in Thy sight.

And then should pride in me arise,
Still on my Saviour fix my eyes;
In Him alone may my trust be
To save my soul eternally.

May I then prove Thy glorious grace
Till free from sin I see Thy face;
Blessing the hand that saved my soul,
I'll sovereign mercy e'er extol.

• For Our Governors •

For those who govern this our land
Oh LORD to Thee we pray,
That they their duties may fulfil
In a God-honouring way.

And though the laws that they decree
Should rule our lives and ways,
May justice in the land be done
And peace known in our days.

But may our rulers be aware
That they will be judged too,
And at God's bar must give account
For things they here did do.

So bless our Queen and all who bear
Rule within this our land;
Oh that they when their lives shall end,
Through Christ may upright stand.

Then will our land be blessed indeed
Through men that honour Thee,
And in this land again we'll know
Of true prosperity.

• For Persecuted Ones •

When in some lands I hear of those
Who trials face from hostile foes,
My prayer would be that such might know
Thy grace, that fortitude they'll show:
For hard they have it, when they stand
For what is right, in many a land:
But if Thy presence they enjoy,
Men will not their true peace destroy.

For then more joy they'll truly know,
Than riches can on men bestow;
Thus though in bondage they may be
And persecutions daily see,
Yet blessings more they'll know indeed
Than those who from such trials are freed;
And though distresses hem them round,
In triumph will their souls abound.

So for these tried ones we would pray,
That help they'll know from day to day,
And where we're blessed with liberty,
May we for this most grateful be:
But those in bonds we'd not forget,
Praying their needs will all be met;
And glad we are, those that oppose,
Will not for ever be their foes,
For those who now in bonds may be
Will soon know wondrous liberty.

• An Evening Prayer •

Another day has quickly gone
And Thy great mercy I must own
Has kept me safe throughout this day
And strengthened me along the way.

As night does fall may I now know
Thy pardoning grace peace to bestow;
As sins committed I confess,
Cloth me with Christ's pure righteousness.

Thou hast this day fed me with bread,
Once more supplied my every need;
How kind Thou art in all Thy ways
And to Thy Name be all the praise.

Throughout this night watch over me,
My great Protector do Thou be;
Refreshing sleep to me afford;
Deal kindly with Thy servant LORD.

And since daybreak will soon be here,
Then by Thy grace do Thou me cheer;
As to my duties I attend,
May I Thee honour to the end.

Thus Thy rich blessing I will prove,
Each day rejoice in Thy great love,
Till ends my life down here below:
Then life eternal shall I know.

• For Forgiveness •

Great God, whose mercy often I
Do see in answered prayer,
I would give thanks, for Thou art kind
And dost to me give ear.

Wilt Thou forgive me for those times
When answers I receive,
Yet in Thy power to bless me so
I lacked faith to believe.

Forgive me too for all the times
When blessings sought I know,
Yet to express my gratitude
I often am so slow.

So humble me my God I pray
And soften my proud heart,
That under Thy correcting rod
I will not have to smart.

And make me conscious of the fact,
Of how much I need Thee;
And how in me there is no good,
That haughty I'll not be.

So may I then in everything
On Thee cast all my care,
And at the last in Heaven above
In wondrous bliss I'll share.

• National Concerns •

LORD when I see within this land
Things which would make me sad,
I look to Thee who can me cheer
And make my heart right glad.

When for my children I'm concerned,
Since sin does them surround,
Then would I pray a time may come
When grace will here abound.

And as so many in our isles
Have turned to heathen ways,
Great God restore us here we pray
And bless us in these days.

For once this land Thy laws observed
And loved the Sabbath Day,
But now so many heed Thee not —
LORD turn their hearts I pray.

So look in mercy, oh my God,
Upon this land I love,
And comfort me in days to come
And grant help from above.

Then will I know of joy and peace
Within my soul and heart,
Which will endure through grief and tears
Since Thou unchanging art.

• REVIVAL •

AT a time of revival, God's Holy Spirit is outpoured in such a way that people in a particular area are made very much aware of how great God is — and how unworthy they are. In Acts 2 we read of a great work when God came down in power and on that day of Pentecost 3,000 were converted. Down through the years there have been many revivals and many of them have affected the whole of the nation.

In East Anglia in 1921 men and women were made so aware of the greatness and holiness of their Creator that fishermen around Lowestoft were overcome by a sense of their sin and the need of a Saviour. Preachers were kept very busy and one who had been formerly despised, found that as he walked through places of work, people were very conscious that they were wrong in God's sight and were now earnestly enquiring about the way of salvation. Many herring girls who had come down from north east Scotland for seasonal work were brought to rejoice in sins forgiven, because of the Gospel of God's free grace, and through this revival (that many have not heard about), Scotland also benefited.

In Wales a revival in 1904 had such effect upon miners that hardened hearts were softened and brought humbly to embrace the truth of the Gospel. It is said that even the pit ponies seemed to notice the difference in their handlers, because swearing and bad language became a thing of the past for many.

It needs to be said that revival is not something which man can bring about, though a spirit of prayer and supplication upon a people often seems to be a forerunner of revival. As we see the need today for such a work in our nation, how good it would be if historians yet to come could say about our times (as it is reported of the 18th century) that through the preaching of the good news of salvation, lives were transformed, drunkenness and immorality curbed, and blessing known in such measure that the whole nation felt the effects of God's mercy and kindness.

• *For Revival* •

Since in this land increasingly
So much that's wrong we see:
We earnestly do plead that here
Revival there might be.

For sin we see on every hand,
Effecting heart and home;
And now like those that call bad good
We sadly have become.

And in our hearts much barrenness
We Thine own people show,
And joy unspeakable in Thee
We very rarely show.

But we look back to days gone by,
When things were very bad,
And mighty preachers were raised up
And many hearts made glad.

For many thousands heard the truth,
When Whitefield made it known;
Souls were from Satan's bondage freed
And his power overthrown.

Then what a difference in our land,
When men their God did fear;
At home, at work, the scene was changed:
Such things we love to hear.

But oh that in this present hour,
Once more Thou wouldst come down,
And may large numbers turn from sin
And Christ their Saviour own.

So look in mercy on our land,
Oh God we humbly pray;
Then bless us richly, and to men
Thy power yet display.

• Proverbs 30:8 •

LORD when prosperity I know,
With health and strength as well,
May I not boast of what I am,
But of Thy mercy tell.

When goods increase and I am blessed
With many earthly things,
Make me aware that these can flee —
Just like a bird with wings.

So LORD I would intreat of Thee
To keep me in that state,
When I will ever honour Thee,
And only on Thee wait.

Then daily may I know Thy grace
To do what pleases Thee;
And, acquiescing in Thy ways,
Sweet providences see.

• For Right Views •

Oh why do I give so much time
To things which soon will be
No more, but pass away, when they
Can no help be to me?

For though I know I have a soul,
Which will live on and on,
When here my body is no more
And earthly pleasure's gone:

Yet still I can so easily
Neglect my deepest need
And live as though I have no soul,
Nor mercy from Thee plead.

So LORD instruct me and give help,
That I will wiser be
Than those who die still unaware
They mercy need from Thee.

And make me know without Thy grace
To hell my soul must go,
Where there is darkness, pain and grief,
And everlasting woe.

And in my heart oh may I know
The joy of sins forgiven,
Through Christ, who died my soul to save
And give me hope of Heaven.

So help me LORD to value more
Those things which matter most:
To love Thy Word and prove its worth —
Not in vain glories boast.

Though thankful for material gifts,
May I them view aright
And wiser be in deeper things,
Nor keep them from my sight.

Then blessed I'll be upon this earth,
But far more blessed above,
Where bliss for ever I shall know,
Through free, eternal love.

• For Missionaries •

Oh LORD for labourers we would pray,
Who work in other lands where they
To many make the Gospel known,
That Satan's power be there put down.

When oft they meet with many foes,
Who would their labour's love oppose,
Then give them strength to labour on;
Through them to Christ may souls be won.

So may false idols be put down,
Then hardened souls the Saviour own;
Thus in dark lands the light will shine
And truths be known which are divine.

LORD, bless Thy labourers overseas
Who've given up much, not seeking ease;
Through them may rich abounding grace
So come to men of other race.

• A Birthday •

Once more another birthday LORD
I have been blessed to see,
And for Thy mercy through my life,
I would give thanks to Thee.

When I look back on the past year,
How quick the days have gone,
Fast as a weaver's shuttle speeds,
As Job to me makes known.

What opportunities I've lost,
Through slothfulness and sin,
When days I've spent in vanity
And I have selfish been.

Yet what amazing kindness Thou
Dost daily show to me,
And for such favours undeserved
May I the humbler be.

And if more days I'm spared to see,
Then give me wisdom LORD,
To pass my days for Thine own praise,
But do Thou help afford.

And where I'm placed may I be blessed
And made a blessing too,
Nor cause Thy Spirit to withdraw,
Through things I wrongly do.

Then my brief life will be enriched
Through things which last for aye,
When some foretastes of things above
I know upon my way.

So on my birthday teach me LORD
To humbly trust Thee more,
And my days number, so my heart
Grows wiser than before.

Then when my birthdays all are o'er
And my turn comes to die,
I'll bless the hand that set me right
For bliss beyond the sky.

• My Heart •

Within my heart, when wrongs arise,
Then LORD God put them down,
Oh may I not let them there dwell,
But grace wilt Thou make known:
So may I follow things which Thou
Hast said do honour Thee,
Then turn away from worldly ways
Which grievous are to Thee.

Make me aware though that my sin
Can only be forgiven
Through Christ, who died to deal with it
When He came down from Heaven:
Then what a wondrous thing to know
My sins on Him were laid,
And His pure righteousness I'm given
And free from guilt I'm made.

So may I not delight in things
Within my heart and mind,
Which caused my Saviour grief to know
Of such a bitter kind:
But greater love may I now show
For mercy shown to me,
Then may I glorify Thee LORD,
Wherever I may be.

• My Tongue •

Oh LORD Thy help I need,
That day by day,
I when my tongue I use,
Might only say
Words that do honour Thee,
And speak Thy praise,
Which flow forth from a heart
That loves Thy ways.

So may I when I speak
Help those I see,
And wrongful ways oppose,
Yet always be
Aware of how I could
Fall by the way:
So may I Thy help know
Both night and day.

Then will I in my ways
True wisdom show,
And cheer to some I'll bring
Whilst here below;
Then when my life is o'er,
Praise I will give,
To Him who died that I
Might ever live.

• MARRIAGE •

THE LORD JESUS said in Matthew 19:4: "Have ye not read, that He which made them at the beginning made them male and female, and said, For this cause shall a man leave father and mother, and shall cleave to his wife: and they twain shall be one flesh?" Also in the Bible we read in Hebrews 13:4: "Marriage is honourable in all, and the bed undefiled: but whoremongers and adulterers God will judge."

• *A Wedding Prayer* •

Great God, as on this happy day,
We in Thy care rejoice,
Our praise to Thee we now would bring
With heart and soul and voice:
For in Thy goodness we now meet
On this blest wedding day
And thank Thee for this bride and groom,
Now met their vows to say.

We thank Thee for Thy kindness when
Thou first to man didst give
An helpmeet, that through love and care
Much joy they might receive;

And we would pray these dear ones here
True love may daily show,
Then through their lives be much enriched
And heavenly blessings know.

So hear our prayer and gracious be,
As these two now become
One flesh, and help them every day,
And bless them in their home;
Then when their journey here is done,
Through Christ then may they know
In Heaven more joy through sins forgiven
Than any felt below.

• A Protestant Prayer •

When evils in this land arise,
Displeasing in Thy people's eyes,
For Thy Word may we stand,
Nor compromise those truths displayed,
As martyrs past were not afraid,
Upheld by Thy strong hand.

And if the Gospel, which alone
Can for our sin and guilt atone,
Despised by some may be;
Still in the truth that Christ here taught,
For which the martyrs nobly fought,
We will stand constantly.

So LORD may we be bold, nor fear
The rage of man while Thou art near,
Who will Thy grace afford;
Then come what may we surely will
Through good o'ercome both wrong and ill,
And stand fast for Thy Word.

• For Our Land •

Great God, whilst judgments on our land,
Through wind and tempest fall,
So work in men that by Thy grace
They will for mercy call.

For sin we see on every hand
As men Thy laws despise,
And in their conduct have no fear
Of God before their eyes.

And those that govern this our land
Of evil ways approve,
And do not heed the warnings given
By One who is above.

And now as man delights in wrong,
Not caring for Thy ways;
Diseases in our land we have
Not seen for many days.

For we are reaping what we've sown
And hence we ought to see,
That sin cannot be trifled with,
But punished it will be.

Yet if repentance we do show
And from our folly turn;
Of pardon through a Saviour's blood,
We happily would learn.

So though great judgment we deserve,
In mercy bless us LORD:
And once again may we become
A land that loves Thy Word.

At the End of the Day

For all the blessings of the day,
My thanks, O LORD, to Thee I pay;
My sins to Thee I now confess
And plead a Saviour's righteousness.

From all my sins may I be washed,
Ere in my bed I soon am hushed,
So if I ne'er again awake,
Mine eyes may on the glory break.

In waking moments fill my mind,
With pleasures of a heavenly kind;
From evil dreams LORD keep me free,
May Satan's power not conquer me.

If for another day I'm spared,
May I at all times honour God.
Help me to stay my mind on Thee
And be from mine own counsels free.

So help me in my times and ways,
Ever to live unto Thy praise,
And when this earth shall be no more,
May I in Heaven Thee adore.

1 Chronicles 29:11-13

To Thee O LORD alone belongs
Greatness and power divine,
Yea, victory and majesty
For ever LORD are Thine.

For all that is in earth below
And in the heaven above,
Is only Thy possession LORD
And cometh from Thy love.

Thou also art the exalted One
Who ruleth in the sky;
Nought can be hidden from the gaze
Of Thine all-seeing eye.

Both wealth and honour come of Thee,
Who rulest over all,
And strength and riches are Thy gifts,
Who makest great and small.

We therefore praise and thank Thee LORD
For all that Thou dost give,
And may we ever thankful be
As long as we shall live.